SEP   2002

"I appreciated *From Fallen to Forgiven* not just as a writer and Christian, but as someone who found this work tremendously encouraging toward deepening my daily walk with the Lord. Ms. O'Neill's presentation of her message—including her own song lyrics and scriptural references—is a comfort and source of strength to which anyone can turn. And return."

—JOHN TINKER
Creator & Producer, "Judging Amy"

"As in our recent women's conference, Jennifer beautifully communicates her love for God and people in the pages of this in-depth, biblically based study. You'll appreciate her refreshing honesty and be changed forever by God's message of forgiveness."

—DR. ROBERT SCHULLER
Founding Pastor, Crystal Cathedral Ministries

"Jennifer has lived many lives in her few years. She shares how her amazing walk with the Lord has healed many wounds. Everyone reading this book will find a common struggle in their own life and they will receive ministering testimony. Her honesty and openness are refreshing."

—MARILYN McCoo
Singer

"Jennifer O'Neill's deeply moving book *From Fallen to Forgiven* is a beautifully written chronicle of one Christian's journey from self-destruction to healing through the power of forgiveness. Learn from her words and know the power of moving beyond our own trespasses and giving those who have trespassed against us back over to God where they rightly belong."

—MICHAEL A. ADAMSE, PH.D.
Clinical Psychologist, Author, Radio Host

"Jennifer O'Neill writes with candor and conviction about the transforming power of forgiveness and the blessings of God's tender mercies. Her compelling story proves that there's no cause so lost, no fear so great, no relationship so bruised that by God's grace it can't be rescued, calmed, and sanctified."

—H. JACKSON BROWN, JR.
Author of Life's Little Instruction Book

"All those who are Christians, weak and strong, should read this book. My reading renewed my faith and love affair with Jesus Christ, Son of the living God!"

—DON PHILLIPS
Academy Award winning Producer & Casting Director

"Jesus said of a certain woman that she loved much because she had been forgiven much. Jennifer O'Neill can say the same. Anyone who thinks she or he is beyond forgiveness should read Jennifer's life story. It is encouraging, uplifting, and beautiful—as she is!"

—CAL THOMAS
Syndicated Columnist

"This book is much more than an amazing testimony. Jennifer provides practical application through God's Word and her own experiences of how to come out of bondage and pain into a brand new life. Jennifer is a frequent guest speaker at Mercy Ministries of America to hurting young women, and her impact on them is immeasurable."

—NANCY ALCORN
President and Founder, Mercy Ministries

"Jennifer O'Neill's life story reminds us that healing is not only possible but promised. Jennifer's journey will enlighten the reader to the fact that God has a plan! A plan of purpose and provision to any and all who seek and offer forgiveness in the name of Jesus Christ."

—DUDLEY C. RUTHERFORD
Pastor, Shepherd of the Hills Church

"Jennifer O'Neill has invited us to embrace the experience of forgiveness and the journey towards wholeness with elegance and a healthy sense of humor. Her penchant for writing is only matched by her passion for God's love. *From Fallen to Forgiven* is a gift at the threshold of the doorway of hope. You'll walk away from this encounter knowing that what was done can be undone."

—DR. MARK J. CHIRONNA
The Master's Touch International Church

"I am absolutely convinced that one of the most important experiences we must endure to become comfortable in God's presence is what Jennifer's book is all about. Jennifer exemplifies the beauty of honest and transparency. I am truly grateful and acknowledge the value of her contributions to the body of Christ as a writer."

—STEPHEN S. SAWYER
Christian Artist, ART for GOD

"By opening up the depths of her own pain and brokenness, she allows us to see the nail-scarred hands of Jesus tenderly pick up the broken pieces of her life, cleansing the shame and healing the pain in a way that moves us all to trust Jesus with our darkest secrets and most painful memories."

—REV. TOMMY HAYS
Messiah Ministries

"Readers will discover an intimate and moving account of a soul's unfolding. For all who wrestle with disappointment, distrust and rejection, this book offers words of encouragement and spiritual insight into the power of forgiveness as a way to calm, to reconcile and to heal."

—CARLA ARCHULETTA
Marketing Consultant

From Fallen to Forgiven

From Fallen to Forgiven

*A Spiritual Journey into
Wholeness and Healing*

JENNIFER O'NEILL

W PUBLISHING GROUP™
www.wpublishinggroup.com
A Division of Thomas Nelson, Inc.
www.ThomasNelson.com

FROM FALLEN TO FORGIVEN

Published by W Publishing Group, a division of Thomas Nelson, Inc., P.O. Box 141000, Nashville,
Tennessee 37214.

Unless otherwise noted, Scripture quotations are from the HOLY BIBLE: NEW INTERNATIONAL
VERSION®. Copyright © 1973, 1978, 1984 by International Bible Society. Used by permission of
Zondervan Publishing House. All rights reserved.

Scripture quotations noted KJV are from the KING JAMES VERSION.

Scripture quotations noted NKJV are from THE NEW KING JAMES VERSION. Copyright © 1979,
1980, 1982, Thomas Nelson, Inc., Publishers.

Library of Congress Cataloging-in-Publication Data

ISBN 0-8499-1715-8

Printed in the United States of America

01 02 03 04 05 BVG 7 6 5 4 3 2 1

To Mom and Dad,
You both have given me many wonderful gifts—
standards, style, and a model of marriage to aspire
to. Thank you for your unwavering support.

Contents

*Be kind and compassionate to one another, forgiving
each other, just as in Christ God forgave you.*

—Ephesians 4:32

*He has taken me to the banquet hall,
and his banner over me is love.*

—Song of Songs 2:4

Introduction

GOD IS LIKE THE WIND. YOU CAN'T SEE HIM, BUT you can see the results of His passing through. Although I have never personally observed someone receive a physical healing and literally "throw away the crutches," God has healed me of more physical, mental, emotional, and spiritual ailments and "crutches" than one person has a right to. It is said in the Bible:

> Then Jesus told him, "Because you have seen me, you have believed; blessed are those who have not seen and yet have believed." (John 20:29)

I imagine it must have been easy for the Israelites to believe in God after Moses parted the Red Sea for them by God's command and power. Who would consider not believing in or following Jesus if we stood with Him as He cast out demons, raised the dead, and healed people before our very eyes? Our lives are full of miracles—the births of our children, the scope and beauty of nature, simply existing within the mystery of our own body's unfathomable design—yet most of the time we feel we've never actually witnessed an honest-to-goodness miracle. Have you ever asked yourself if it's crazy to believe God can heal our deepest, darkest hurts? Have we spent years praying for healings without receiving them? Are we insane to keep trying? I don't know about you, but I've always thought healing all my messes would require a miracle or ten! So what's new now?

For me, the answer to that question came in a wave of revelations at every whistle-stop town along my way to wholeness. As with my conversion to Christ, my understanding of God's process of complete healing was revealed to me in slow-motion increments. (I have come to love the drama of God's choreography!)

LOVE AT FIRST SIGHT

Over the last year I had started to work on a book for preteen girls titled "Love at First Sight." I was full tilt in creative mode and enjoying myself immensely. The thrust of the book was to connect the unique, deep-rooted love so many girls have for horses to the love Jesus has for them. As I worked on the project, it took me back to a past of sweet, youthful memories. I jotted down a fanciful vision because sometimes it's good for the soul to remember the "little girl" in us all.

MY HORSE
When I was eight years old, I could fly down the stairs leading
   from my bedroom to the landing below.
On the wings of a prayer, I was airborne . . . I swear.
Once outside, beyond the confines of skeptical eyes,
I bound along with lightning speed—my foot never in need of the
   grassy slopes. I was free.

*Through the woods I raced, all obstacles I faced fell far
 behind . . .*
*Like waves drawn to shore, my rhythm was kept in perfect
 time—in my mind I was unstoppable.*
Relieved of logic or what was taught in school,
I was cool . . . a new breed!
And the only one that could fly with me was my horse.
Surefooted and true to course, we were never afraid—
*An awesome force to contend with . . . and in the end, we conquered
 the very highest places and faced the world below as one . . .*
My horse—my hero—my friend . . .

I don't believe I've ever met a little girl who doesn't flat-out fall head-over-heels for horses. That instant, almost mysterious adoration of the animal quickly evolves into a unique relationship worthy of exploration and protection. "Love at First Sight" is a chronicle for "girls of all ages" whose coming of age takes shape against the backdrop of snuggly ponies and heroic horses. The book celebrates the love affair with horses alongside encouragement and real answers for teens struggling with self-esteem, the need for affirmation, and the pressures of growing up whole in today's crazy world. I was so excited about this uplifting project and the effect it might have on young women—especially after hearing so many horror stories from worried moms and unhappy teens during my teaching seminars.

Then, out of the blue, I received a call from the W Publishing Group requesting a meeting. Wow. They offered me a book contract! "Thank You, God," I squealed like the preteens I was writing for—"Love at First Sight" would be published! God, however, had different timing in mind. The publishers put my girls' book on hold, eager instead to have me write about my last fifteen years as a Christian, and to chronicle my spiritual journey of ups and downs since I came to Christ. I prayed about it. Then I had to pray some more. My girl's book had an incredible message of God's love, and I didn't understand why it shouldn't be published first. I was disgruntled that the schedule I had envisioned didn't seem to line up with God's, but I finally submitted to His timing, assured in prayer that the "Love at First Sight" book was not lost, just postponed.

PIECE BY PIECE

Since it wasn't clear to me exactly what God did want me to write next, I found myself in that uncomfortable "one-door-closes before-the-next-one-opens" phase. Having been there before, I knew there was no way to hurry the process or force the issue, so I gave up and waited on God. That's always a tough one for me! I reminded myself that God might just be pulling off one of His "almighty turns of events" and I should just try to live up to the pact I'd recently made with Him to stop arguing with every directive of the Holy Spirit!

With my girls' book shelved for the moment, I started to piece together my presentation for this book. "Piece by piece" would better describe the process, because *nothing* was flowing. In fact, God was not going to reveal His book to me until He worked *me* through its message. If I had known what I was in for, I probably would have called upon one of a hatful of excuses to politely decline what in fact was God's invitation to attend my own healing party. As it was, God simply plunked me into the middle of my flawed personality mix, chained to my past by my bevy of nasty issues, and stirred the whole mess around for a bit of disclosure. Ooooh . . . and ouch!

I began the outline of the book's depth and width, which, by the way, have been changing up until this very moment of writing to you. After I reviewed my Bible study from the year before, the most glaring lessons expressed in my notes were for me to prioritize my life for God and to put Him first in all I did, with an increasing focus on His Word and will. From that perspective, I titled the book, "Lord of My Life." I was inspired since the fruits of that year's study had already afforded me improvements, beginning with my relationship with Jesus, as well as areas of growth evident in my marriage, my family, my ministry, and my personal peace. The publishers were also pleased with the "Lord of My Life" message, and I felt sure that I was on my way to what God wanted me to write next. Nope, I only had part of it right.

FORGIVENESS AND HEALING

As I continued to work on the book, I was also preparing a three-hour seminar on healing for a church in Jackson, Tennessee, where I had recently acted in a stage play. I titled the seminar series "The Heart of the Matter," and when the speaking engagement arrived, the Holy Spirit led me through the text with revelations and directions I had never prepared for or anticipated! It was a clear and unwavering request by God to expand the message of "Lord of My Life" to include "Healing the Heart of the Matter." I went back to my publishers, and they were also excited about the additions. I was thankful to be aligned with such a formidable publishing company whose priority was to get God's message out, no matter how many title changes I went through.

I began to focus the text on the overwhelming need for healing in all our lives. By the way, I am never in a roomful of women, churched or not, without knowing in my heart that I am surrounded by many with unresolved, unforgiven, unhealed issues. The battle scars cover areas from abortion, sexual abuse, unfulfilled and deceitful relationships of all kinds, to anger, depression, and addictions, all wrapped up in denials of every flavor. The need for all of us to recognize our hurts and heal these areas is imperative for a healthy, happy, spiritually successful life of wholeness and purpose. But how? I wanted healing for myself as well as for every woman sitting in front of me. I wanted healing for my children, my family, and my friends. I wanted healing for people I might never meet personally. More importantly, God says He wants healing for every one of His children. It was then that He showed me how, and the title of the book was once and for all changed to *From Fallen to Forgiven*. Forgiveness and healing are God's desires and message to all of us!

As soon as I started writing, I found myself cast as the leading lady in a string of new nightmarish experiences. These haunting dreams plagued my sleep in an effort to thwart my next mission of writing by undermining my resolve. The nightly Technicolor epics were frightening reenactments of dark places and secrets I obviously still carried deep within. Yes, I had finally reached the point of realization that God didn't have perspiration on His upper lip about me, but it was also apparent that I was not immune to the enemy's onslaughts aimed to throw me off track. Satan and his little band of demon-thieves didn't like that I was about to embark on God's crash course of cleaning out my areas of unforgiveness, which would bring me healing. The dark side preferred me bound with diminished capacity, and it most definitely did not want me to share the good news of release with others.

Be self-controlled and alert. Your enemy the devil prowls around like a roaring lion looking for someone to devour. (1 Peter 5:8)

Still, I do not want to give the enemy too much credit.

If God is for us, who can be against us? (Romans 8:31)

The one who is in you is greater than the one who is in the world. (1 John 4:4)

Several years ago when I went through the process of writing my autobiography, *Surviving Myself*, I had to revisit the good, the bad, and the superugly of my past, and in doing so, God began to cleanse and redirect my life toward His will, grace, and blessings. Since I was—and always will be—a "work in progress," God's work in me wasn't complete. He wanted a more thorough healing so I could further reach my potential in Him. None of us can give what we don't have, and we can't have what we have not received. According to God's Word, I needed to give forgiveness so I would have His forgiveness. Then I could receive His healing, and I could recycle God's incredible message of love back . . . to you to pass on. That's what this book is all about.

SURVIVING MYSELF

I had the looks—to get my way
I had it down—just what to say
Grew up so fast—nothing much lasted
Rehashing the bad—reliving the sadness
Rehearsing my lines—only to find
I was blazing a sorry path

Since I was a girl—out in the world
Looking for someone to love me
Caught in a lie—compromised
I never looked above me
I needed help—surviving myself
Lord, I needed help—surviving myself

I found the touch—on a full moon night
I had his ring on my finger—but he didn't treat me right
The emptiness—I couldn't fill it
I was willing to change—but not pay the price
I was learning the hard way—that life's not so nice
And all the pain—I couldn't kill it

Since I was a girl—out in the world
Looking for someone to love me
Caught in a lie—compromised
I never looked above me
I needed help—surviving myself
Lord, I needed help—surviving myself

Looked like I had it all
Looked like I had it made
But in my shame
I was too afraid to call Your name

But there You were, Lord,
Right where You've always been
Calling my name—forgiving my sin
Giving me hope—showing me love
I was floating on air—wrapped in Your hug
I'm sharing my heart—starting again
I found my Savior—my friend

Since I was a girl—out in the world
Looking for someone to love me
Caught in a lie—compromised
I never looked above me
I needed help—surviving myself

WORDS AND MUSIC BY JENNIFER O'NEILL.
HANDSHAKE PRODUCTIONS.
USED BY PERMISSION.

I

Surviving Myself

Finding God Between the Lines

Wherever you are . . . so is God.

—J. O'N

"LOOKING FOR LOVE IN ALL THE WRONG PLACES" WAS the hook line of a melody that held the dubious distinction of being my life's theme song. That was until fifteen years ago when I finally experienced my first real love affair with Jesus Christ . . . a love that would forever change my tune.

SURVIVING MYSELF

At the prompting of my children, I wrote my autobiography in 1998. Frankly, I couldn't help but be amused at how appropriate *Surviving Myself* was as the title to my life's story—a life that looked fantastic on the outside, but in truth, was tormented within. Why? How does one share equal time with a list of credits including modeling, money, movies, and international acclaim with a rap sheet of near-death experiences, sexual abuse, multiple marriages, and misfortune? "Fasten your seat belt" comes to mind right about now.

While I took on the world, it courted me with jet-set speed

1

and every seduction that money, travel, fame, and global diversities could promise. Friends and suitors came and left my life according to my financial status and appearances on the "World's Most Beautiful" or "Box Office Most Wanted" lists. From an outcast grade schooler, I grew as a working teen into a taller package who was instantly supposed to have it all together. "Instantly" took me most of my life.

Today, at age fifty-three, I continue to be successful in my work, but more important, in Christ I have found balance as a wife, daughter, friend, mother of three (Aimee, 32; Reis, 21; Cooper, 14), and grandmother of three. Not unlike a horse that's not been cooled down after expending extreme effort, I have all too often felt, as we say in riding circles, "rode hard and put away wet." But I am happy to report that, despite myself, I am finally winning God's race by faith and not by my own brawn. Still, before I take you on a victory lap, let me fill you in on just some of the details of why I now get up every morning of my life with a sense of awe and gratitude at God's amazing patience, grace, and mercy.

ME, MYSELF, AND I

Within the first decade of my life I had a catalog of magical secrets that I shared only with me, myself, and I (my three best friends). The most impressive achievements in my repertoire were my abilities to fly at will or vanish at a moment's notice. Not even Michael, my older brother by sixteen months, was privy to my star qualities of flight and fancy, since I only performed these masterful tricks in the privacy of my mind. You see, having "me" as my ever-appreciative audience seemed more and more the only way I could feel good about myself, although it wasn't always that way. There were those times when my parents hosted one of their famous gatherings of eat, drink, and be merry, and I would boldly venture where no one else dared. I'd dance right through their party like a whirling dervish to the delight of live late-night applause. The guests were thoroughly wowed! I'm convinced it was the showmanship of those evenings that birthed my lifelong penchant for performing. Carefree and unencumbered, I was full of colorful dreams and grand schemes as a young girl. Innocent of disappointments, I believed that everything was possible, and that the world was fair, as well as fair game. I was unstoppable—until rejection entered stage right . . .

My first memories of feeling "invisible" are from age ten, following my family's move from the suburbs of New York City to the Connecticut countryside. It was then that my life took its initial turn for the worst. I quickly realized that it was one thing to play a great game of hide-and-seek when it was my choice to blend into the woodwork or become one with a pile of laundry, but it was quite another to feel unheard, unimportant, and unlovable. It seems one's sense of personal worth takes shape in childhood, usually beginning with our parents' influence, and although my family has given me *many* wonderful things, the sense of being valued as a child was not one of them. Yes, "invisible" is a good description of how I felt at my core, a deficit that was to haunt me for most of my life. This feeling, however, didn't affect the ease with which I would later attend dinners at the White House or travel the world—it was more of a personal parasite that preyed on the matters of my heart.

A LOVE STORY

My mom and dad have always been madly in love, with fifty-six years of successful marriage to show for it. Their attraction ignited like a bonfire when they first met at a Key Club in London during World War II. Mom (Irene Frieda Lillian Pope) was a classic English beauty from a large family of little means and great dreams. The man I call Dad is known to others by the wonderful culturally diverse name of Oscar Delgado O'Neill Jr. My father was a twenty-four-year-old "ace" captain pilot—a war hero with a capital *H*. When he first laid his fiery eyes on his nineteen-year-old bride-to-be, a new chapter was penned in the annals of romance.

Oscar was born of privilege and sported international savoir-faire and multilingual charm. On their third date, Dad asked "Rene," as he calls her, for her hand, and just as life was about to imitate cinema, Dad was shot down over Germany on his second-to-last mission. He remained in prison camp for the next two and a half years. Once released, Dad returned to London, married Mom, and whisked her away to Rio de Janeiro, Brazil, where my brother and I were born.

I'm boastfully proud of my intriguing birthplace as well as my parents' story of passion and style; a tale I've told always with great gusto. But there were some downsides to Mom and Dad's lusty yet volatile dedication to each other. One of them was the fact that my brother and I were unwittingly pitted against each other for our parents' attention (which they reserved solely for each other). Mind you, this was not malicious on their part, just the consequence of where they placed "children" in the scheme of their lives together. Although dinner was always on the table growing up, that didn't soothe the carnage of my parents' almost nightly drink and song, often ending in my mother's threats of divorce laced with her expressions of discontent. Mom was someone you took very seriously, but Mike and I eventually learned that her divorce threats were just her way of venting frustration.

For the most part, Mom's anger was born of my dad's extensive business travel. Mom was left alone a lot when Mike and I were young, and she didn't like it a lick. Consequently, when Dad was home, he was, is, and always will be all hers. Mom disallowed me more and more of my father, and he easily acquiesced, never offering any personal attention or alone time for either me or Mike. Never. For me, the sibling contest for their recognition resulted in a powerfully destructive dose of low self-esteem. I quickly became an overachiever in an effort to earn my parents' love and favor. When straight A's and polite behavior didn't do the trick, a deep-seated fury was planted in my soul, one that would rear its ugly head whenever I felt unloved. This marked the beginning of my "negative tape," which sent me a message of an inevitable future of worthlessness and doom. It was then that I began to feel what was to become that all-too-familiar ache in my heart: the unidentified emptiness and painful yearning that was not to be filled by anyone until I accepted Jesus Christ into my life so many years later.

Mike and I grew apart, casualties of our bids for affirmation. I always yearned for a protective big brother, but instead, Mike and I seemed only to be able to take out our personal pain on one another.

Entering my teens, I attended dancing school (white gloves and all), never made cheerleader (couldn't do the splits or play the girly game), ran the fastest mile in the entire girls' high school in ninth grade, and was ruthlessly labeled "flat-chested" by my brother. Mike was so good at his self-appointed mission of demoralizing me that he actually succeeded in making permanent tread marks on my sense of security. Not one to ever give up, I formulated a retort: "Well, Mike, you have flat feet, so there!" My less than brilliant barb didn't seem to bother him in the slightest. Nonetheless, today I have the last laugh knowing I grew out of my "flat," while Mike still has his!

FEAR

Fear took an early foothold in my life; I had a rampaging gorilla as a recurring nightmare for far too many years. My gorilla wasn't like King Kong, with a loving heart for his heroine. Mine ravaged the neighborhood as he violently made his way past every imaginable obstacle in his search for me. At night, I would spend what seemed an eternity in my pitch-black room frantically searching the walls for the door to the hall. Mom and Dad wouldn't let us leave the lights on in our rooms at bedtime, and on occasions when I became thoroughly frightened of the dark and made my way out of my room, I would be found downstairs sleepwalking or sitting huddled in a corner. As a youngster, the sound of thunder also found me cowering under the kitchen table in a hysterical state. I've always wondered what triggered such terror in me.

FOUR-LEGGED FRIENDS

I began to live more and more in a fantasy world of hidden gardens and animals as my only friends and support team. My escape, however, merely led to more frustration as my parents were unilaterally disinterested and disapproving of my passion for animals. According to Mom and Dad, "Horses, dogs, and cats are merely a young girl's yearning, a phase Jennifer will quickly outgrow." Today, I enjoy a good chuckle with my parents (who have lived with me for the last eight years) when we look out of their living-room window at my farm, and all they see are horses, dogs, and cats. We certainly have come full circle.

Fueling passions that refused to be quenched, I managed to find a neighbor's broken-down horse, which I took care of in exchange for some rides. By some miracle I also talked my parents into allowing me to keep an outdoor cat my aunt had given me. His name was Groucho. It was only after Groucho birthed a set of kittens that Mom and Dad realized "he" was a "she." The courtship of my cat by the local toms irritated my parents, so they took Groucho to the animal shelter, countering my objections with a dog I named Mandy. I never stopped hating myself for giving in to their bribe of a dog in exchange for a cat—as if they were trading cards. In reality, there was nothing I could do about their decision, but that fact didn't ease my feelings of remorse. In my heart, I was a traitor, simple as that.

Not long after Mandy arrived she was run over by a car. I was sure I was being punished by her death and swore I would never give up on an animal again. The endless list of strays and ailing and aging pets I have tirelessly cared for over the years is a result of that childhood guilt as much as of my pure love for animals. When I was thirteen, Mom and Dad did get me another dog, a puppy that I also called Mandy in honor of "Mandy One," but it wasn't long before I would lose her, too, *and* everything else I held near.

THE END OF MY WORLD

At fourteen, my parents sent my brother off to boarding school, then promptly announced to me that we were moving to Manhattan. Obviously, my horse had to be left behind, but I begged them to allow me to at least take my dog along. Their answer was an unequivocal "No." With that, my world ended. I know now that I didn't *really* want to die, I just wanted to be heard. I wanted Mom and Dad to recognize that my dog meant everything to me. She was all I had. She was my only friend. She loved me, just the way I was. I ended up swallowing my mother's bottle of sleeping pills, one by one, and went outside to lie next to Mandy so I could hold her when I faded away. That's what it felt like, just slipping off into nothingness where the pain finally stopped. If I wasn't around anymore, maybe "they" would miss me. Maybe "they" would finally take me seriously. Maybe "they" would know how much they hurt me. Have you ever hurt yourself because no one else could see how much pain you were in?

My attempted suicide was the first of many close calls, ranging from car accidents to being shot. Despite my turns with danger, God had His arms around me, protecting me from my sin, my sadness, and Satan, who was vying for my soul before I was to personally know my Savior. This battle was an ongoing one with eternal consequences weighing in the balance. With every fall, the drama broadened and the stakes got higher.

Mom and Dad called my cry to be heard a "stunt," and off we went to Manhattan, leaving Mandy behind. My pain was shoved down into a deep, dark place, and was never recognized, understood, grieved, or healed. Moving into survival mode, my tenacious side kicked in and I decided I was now on a mission for independence. I attended Dalton, a private girls' school in the city, maintained A's, and through a series of amazing events, started modeling at age fifteen. The modeling scared me to pieces because I was so shy, but I talked my parents into letting me work because I was so determined to buy my own horse. For me, modeling was just a means to an end. If I had to make my own dreams come true, so be it. It was during that time that my pattern of denying my feelings was established. My "negative tape" just kept getting longer and longer, and I was about to become my own worst enemy.

ALL GROWN UP AND STILL NOWHERE TO GO

As a teenager I was splashed all over international magazine covers and wooed and pursued by movie stars, millionaires, legendary lawyers, flesh-peddling agents, and just plain old bad guys. Since my childhood was a study in emotional neediness, I was courting trouble. Against all odds, traditional family structure appealed to me despite the explosion in the late sixties of "free love" lifestyles and attitudes. Defying my already rising share of damaging physical and emotional onslaughts, I yearned for what I thought would be the safety of a husband. I was convinced that if I were to marry, surely I would be adored just as my father adored my mother, therefore filling that nagging hole in my heart. That dream, I found out, was not to be for this seventeen-year-old bride. I married the first "love of my life" and welcomed my daughter, Aimee, eighteen months later. A divorce followed after six volatile years, framed by my surging movie career. I became a study in extremes.

In my twenties, I worked in Europe, dabbled in film editing, traveled the world, saw my movies open at the Cannes and Deauville Film Festivals, and won multiple international and U.S. awards for acting. I also did my photography show, painted oil portraits, bred and showed my horses, signed a record deal, and developed a nightclub act, yet I seemed more confounded by relationships as I turned thirty than I did at twenty. My career soared with such movie hits as *Summer of '42, Rio Lobo,* and *Scanners,* but my personal life progressively fell apart. My next attempt at true love brought with it a scar that I thought would never heal . . .

I had been engaged to an extremely powerful man for two years when I became pregnant. I was ecstatic at the idea of having a child with my fiancé, a man I loved so and was finally about to marry. My joy was short-lived as I stood frozen in horror and disbelief at his unequivocal negative response to my "good news." In short, he promised that he would do everything in his power to emotionally and verbally coerce me into getting an abortion. If I insisted on carrying the baby, he swore he would take "his" baby away from me—and assured me, in a tone of voice I had never heard him use before, that he had the political clout, financial means, and industry power to annihilate me personally and professionally.

CHOICES

In the seventies we were told a lie from the pit of hell (and it is still told today), that a pregnancy is just a blob of tissue in the uterus up until three months' gestation. We have no moral responsibility to a blob of tissue—that microscopic entity without a name or a face is no one. Everyone, including my mom and dad and my doctor, told me that abortion of the "tissue" prior to three months' maturity was "all right"—just an inconvenience. Ignorance on my part is a weak excuse, but an accurate one. I now feel that, despite all the overwhelming outside pressure, I was pitiful in my inability to stand up against others' reasoning, no matter how powerful. I buckled under fear. I didn't know then where to find real strength, to find real truth. Deep down I knew I was wrong to abort my baby, even when everyone was saying it was right. Nothing in the world could ever make me opt for that choice again. I hated myself. And I hated what I had done.

My quest for love and acceptance continued and directed me through many more marriages, each of which I was convinced would last forever. Clearly, when you don't value yourself, you're

not likely to attract anyone who does, and codependent relationships became my trademark. "If you ever leave me, I'm going
with you" was my unspoken "M.O.," and by age thirty-eight, I
had mourned nine miscarriages (certain that they were punish-
ments for my abortion), multiple brushes with death, numerous
broken limbs including my neck and back, car crashes, a gunshot
wound, life-threatening surgeries, defaulted multimillion-dollar
contracts, and early bouts with depression resulting in hospitali-
zation and shock therapy. My choices in men left me with severe
trust issues exacerbated by verbal batterings as I wrestled with
the eventual discovery of their various affairs, and theft culmi-
nating in the loss of my home and all my assets. Nothing, however, was as devastating as the years of deception that finally led
to the exposure of one of my husbands' sexual abuse of my
daughter.

Twenty years ago I had never heard of "sexual abuse." The
subject wasn't on the daily news, and it certainly wasn't dinner-
table conversation. I had never known anyone who had been
sexually abused, nor did I know anyone who had even peripher-
ally dealt with sexual abuse. The fact was, I didn't have a clue
that my daughter had been abused. Was I just plain stupid, or
was my husband just a brilliant con artist? Maybe a little of both.
Oh, how I tortured myself with those questions! The eventual
accusation by my daughter that my husband had been sexually
abusing her for four years, and his staunch "lie-detector safe"
denial of that accusation led to a whole year of closed family
court hearings. At the end of that year I had lost my home, my
husband, and my daughter, suffered a gunshot wound, and nearly
died on two separate occasions due to medical complications.

As I was lying in a hospital bed in 1982 recovering from the
doctor's surgical bid to try to put "Humpty Dumpty Jennifer"

back together again, I considered the .38-caliber wound that had entered my abdomen and exited through my hip bone about as dramatic and traumatic as the "soppy soaps" I was mindlessly staring at on TV. Yes, I would heal, but emotional recovery was not to be on my immediate agenda. I became fresh meat for the international media with their speculations of what was going on in my previously quiet, un-Hollywood life. In *Surviving Myself* I detail how I was accidentally shot and then (due to legal issues) was not allowed to address the hounding press with the real areas of stress and pain in my life. I was put through the judicial system for possession of an unregistered weapon when I was the one who was shot! It was not my gun, but still I was bound to silence by "sealed court orders" and by my choice of nondisclosure of my then husband (for the sake of our son). I felt like a scapegoat. It was unjust. It was also my first spin with what I call the "big machines." I was out of control. Life was out of control. And still God had His hand on my shoulder waiting for me to turn to Him.

Both husband and wife can usually take credit for a failed marriage, and for my part, my need to be loved made me emotionally unstable at the hands of rejection as I searched for ways to numb my anger. With every one of their lies and my resulting disappointment and hurt, I became more obnoxious, depressed, and dramatic. At the same time I was extremely driven and resilient. Consequently, my highs as well as my lows were excessively intense.

CHANGES

They say change comes from pain. I believe it. I always had a feeling of real urgency in my life, yet before I found Christ, my intrinsic pace and course felt more like an uncontrollable avalanche than a designed grand plan. Women may relate to those last few pushes of childbirth when contractions overwhelm that purposeful, controlled breathing and you "lose it" to all-consuming, unrelenting pain—that's out of control! Amazingly, we go back for more birthing and bigger families because once we see that newborn baby, that miracle in our arms, love takes over and all pain is forgotten. Amazing grace! Once I accepted Christ as my Savior, I quickly found out that my "walk" was only beginning, and that being a Christian *wasn't* going to be a "walk in the park."

Over the last fifteen years, I've battled some of my toughest obstacles and opponents. Every button of insecurity, fear, and vulnerability has been and continues to be pushed by some of those very "big machines" who claim to be in charge of my life. All comfort zones and hiding places I have clung to in the past have methodically been removed and replaced by a hard-won new order of priorities. It is clear to me that my ability to handle life's most threatening chapters is in direct correlation to the presence, focus, and strength of my faith. My willingness to sub-mit to God's authority, accept His unimaginable love for me, for-give and be forgiven, and heal and claim the place God has carved out for me has been a journey of a lifetime. Or perhaps, more to the point, will be my lifetime's journey.

It's a relief to finally get to the point at which, despite whatever continuing discomfort I experience, I know that what I hold to be truly valuable in my life is not up for sale, not up for negotiation, and will not be intimidated or destroyed. I look back over my fifty-three years and am astounded by the circuitous route I have taken to happiness and peace. The places I have been, people I have known, things I have learned, and the mountains I have climbed from lowly places I have fallen continue to be nothing less than mind-boggling to me. It's almost beyond comprehension that I managed to never lose my enthusiasm or drive for life or, for that matter, that I eluded cynicism. I am grateful for God's gift of the love that survives in my heart and my desire for the truth. I regret not one detail of my past, as incredibly embarrassing and painful as many may have been, because miraculously, they have all brought me to the present, and into the presence of Christ. I remain humbled and thankful for all my blessings.

What God has had in store for me from the beginning of time is beyond my wildest childhood dreams and imagination. I have experienced His unconditional love in so many ways, not the least of which has been learning to engage the Holy Spirit as not just a hospital to repair and comfort my soul, but as an army of protection and direction! God's blessings in my life supersede Christmas mornings, go beyond the high of my first hurdle on a horse, the births of my children, promises of love, conquering of fears, and attaining ultimate goals. I am believing like it's the first time and I am loving like I've never been hurt before. His gracious restoration of me has become a daily miracle unfolding before my very eyes.

It's not easy to jot down one's history in a single chapter. For that matter, it was difficult enough to try to track the highs and the lows of my life that "looked so good and hurt so bad" in an entire autobiography. By the way, my mom (who is a master of the English language) would critique my last phrase as follows: "Jen, it's 'looked so good and hurt so *badly.*'" And I'd say, "That's too formal for a *song lyric,* Mom." Of course, she's correct, and I thank her for every good manner and correct lingo I've ever mustered. Oops, that wasn't terribly lyrical or correct, was it?

Above all, I thank God that He allowed me chance-after-mistake-after-chance to receive His saving grace. I've come to realize that He loved me enough to sometimes leave me where I was so I would grow in Him. In His arms, every day that I live becomes my forgiven past by night, and a new beginning by the light of dawn. Wow.

FOR ME AND YOU

He knows me, and still He loves me
He goes with me everywhere
Especially when I'm scared
Jesus died for me and you
He's telling the truth, He shows us how to love
He's the way

I found Him in time to stay around Him
My heart would have closed down
Without Him
Jesus Died for me and you
He'll always see us through, He shows us how to love
He's the way

Pray to Him, come on and let Him in
Hear His voice, make the choice, He's Lord

He saved me, He remade me
He told me He'd always be there
When life's unfair
Jesus died for me and you
He's telling the truth, He shows us how to love
He's the way

Jesus died for me and you
He'll always see us through, He shows us how to love
He's the way

WORDS BY JENNIFER O'NEILL
MUSIC BY MERVIN LOUQUE

2

Lord of My Life

Coming to Faith and Leaving the Rest Behind

What moves us past the possibility of failure? Heart!
—J. O'N

HALOED BY A DISTANT SETTING SUN, MY HAIR *flowed about my illuminated face in the slowest of motion. Radiant with anticipation, I extended my arms toward the object of affection, my chiffon dress swirling behind like a bridal train of crystal light. Every captured moment of emotion was accentuated by the slow shutter speed that framed my journey. My eyes brimmed with tears of joy, taking what seemed an eternity to fall from my cheeks as I made my way toward my love . . .*

For me, coming to the Lord felt like a valentine wrapped in a slow-motion Clairol commercial. Some people can remember the very instant they recognized the truth of Jesus Christ in their lives—the time, date, occasion—every detail. The moment of receiving eternal salvation hits most people like a freight train, its initial impact indelibly etched on their hearts, minds, and souls. My experience of coming to Christ seemed to unfold in stages. The evolution began fourteen years ago with what felt like a spiritual world war battling my conversion every step of the way.

Skeptics will say that turning to God is only a result of "hitting bottom with no place left to go," but in my case, at age thirty-eight, I was actually experiencing one of the happiest times of my life. My daughter, Aimee, was twenty and married, Reis was six, and I was pregnant with Cooper (after nine miscarriages). I was also married to a man with whom I was madly in love (*madly* being the operative term!). In keeping with my history of codependent relationships, this marriage was not based on solid ground.

Richard was a handsome Vietnam vet, an ex–rodeo cowboy with a rage apparently born of debilitating posttraumatic stress syndrome from his war experiences, which at that time had gone undiagnosed. His verbal battering, set against my emotional instability, annihilated any hope of our sharing a successful partnership. In addition, what seemed out of step with Richard's temper was the fact that he had been a Christian since childhood, his faith held deep within and rarely evident in the midst of his anger. Despite his apparent incongruities, Richard would intermittently witness to me, encourage me to read the Bible, and pray for my enlightenment. I am eternally thankful to him for that as well as to many others whom I have come to learn prayed for my salvation long before I received Christ.

ENCOURAGEMENT

I talk at length in my autobiography about Eleanor C. Lee, my aunt by marriage, my godmother, and an angel sent to me before I ever believed in angels. Elle was my mom's dear friend, a partner in business with my dad, and for me as a child, the only person who ever made time for just me. We'd play cards; she'd talk to me about God. She left me her piano when she died. I cannot tell you what that meant to me. I used to go to her apartment and plunk away as a kid, and she would sit and listen to my sour notes as if I were playing Beethoven. I moved her piano around with me over the next thirty years of my life, until it literally fell apart. Elle encouraged me, was my mentor, and through her extraordinary heart and caring for others was the best model of Christ I have ever had the honor of knowing. As a child, she planted a seed in me for the love of God by her actions and example, and I thank God for each moment of her influence and presence in my life. I've seen firsthand how the planting of even the smallest mustard seed can grow, with a little watering, into a giant faith, albeit years and years later!

Not only did I have Richard's leadings to the Word and Elle's seed and nurturing, but I also had strangers praying for me for years prior to my ever meeting them as brothers and sisters in faith. In particular, I love to tell the story of the Chrisagises—a family who were an immense influence on my life before I even knew them. According to Marguerite Chrisagis, in 1976 she told her two sons, Brian and Shawn, that she had received a word from the Lord to pray for Jennifer O'Neill. At the time, all they knew was that Jennifer O'Neill was an actress, but their mother was adamant that God had spoken to her audibly to pray for the salvation of this actress. The family faithfully followed that directive—it became their mission. They prayed daily and without question, truly believing that standing firm on God's promises would bring me into a personal relationship with Christ through their faithful intercession. It wasn't until 1995 when they saw my appearance on the *700 Club* show talking about my faith that they realized God had answered their prayers.

Today, the Chrisagises are close friends, work with me on many projects, and our two families have become like one.

I know in my heart and soul that diligent, loving prayers, sometimes from complete strangers, were the catalysts for having Christ in my life today. It is absolutely awesome that God has bestowed such power and eternal significance to our prayers, which in turn give us love and hope for the lost. It's such an honor to be a part of God's Great Commission on both the giving and the receiving end!

Once I accepted Christ as my Savior, I was blessed with many Christian friends and a ravenous appetite for more and more of what I had waited forever for—the saving, transforming, eternal love of Christ. Viva, my dear friend, shared the joys of sisterhood with me before I even knew we were "related" under God. Before I came to the Lord, she spent hours talking to me about Christ while I was searching for answers in my life. I was also significantly encouraged by one wonderful gentleman in particular who had known the Lord since he was a child. He was born to a family of believers, had received miraculous healings, was studied and versed in God's Word, and had the time and wherewithal to walk me through my endless streams of questions, study, and searching of God's wisdom and knowledge. He would do so with the ease in which a mature Christian can lead an impatient fledgling in the knowledge of Christ. When God says He has a plan for each and every one of us, He does. There are teachers, leaders, warriors, intercessors, prophets, mentors, guidance counselors, encouragers, interpreters—the list is endless. Not even one ingredient can be left out of the recipe for spiritual growth, and in the case of bringing a believer along, there can never be too many cooks in the kitchen. When I look back at the "care packages" God sent me, those who lifted me up until I became strong enough to stand in my faith, all I can say is glory be to God, and thank you one and all!

TESTING

When Richard and I dedicated our newborn Cooper, I was baptized and Richard was rebaptized. I was a typical newly saved Christian full of explosive joy and excitement over the prospect of hope, faith, and grace in my life. But being a baby in my faith, I didn't have a clue how to apply my belief to everyday life. I quickly realized that thirty-eight years of worldly living, habits, and damaged perceptions were not going to disappear easily. Satan may have lost the battle for my eternal soul, but he had a deep-rooted hold on my flesh that he guarded with every deceit he could muster. I've learned that salvation is not instantly accompanied by sanctification or the renewing of our minds. Clearly, my journey was just beginning.

My faith was tested right off, on several fronts. I discovered my husband Richard's infidelity, and he decided to leave our marriage. Divorced again, it took me what felt like forever to realize his sexual addiction was not a personal reflection on me, but rather behavior resulting from his past and his inability to have a sustaining relationship with a woman. I say this not as my personal opinion, but rather based on studies of those who suffer from posttraumatic stress syndrome. When Richard was recently diagnosed, he sent me literature on the disease that explained some of the devastating emotional and relational whiplash the syndrome can cause. When I read about it, I felt as if someone had "bugged" our marriage and printed it out in a brochure. At that time, the years of his berating rages mixed with my lifelong scroll of insecurities wrapped me in another serious bout of depression in spite of the fact that I had Jesus in my heart. I felt betrayed and abandoned again.

Estranged for so long from the residue of a list of "mother/daughter" issues topped by the sexual abuse she suffered, Aimee and I struggled, often unsuccessfully, to repair our relationship. We were like fallen prey fighting for a breath as the enemy tore at our throats; the wounds were deep and continued to bleed. As years passed and I came to my faith, we also did not share Christ as a common denominator. Today we speak entirely different languages and take diverse approaches in resolving our mutual pain. I believe, for the most part, that "communication" fuels our stalemate. Despite the obstacles, we have always longed for and missed each other terribly, enjoying periods of closeness, but not ultimate victory as yet.

In the beginning, Aimee was cautious of my Christianity. Although she made it clear that I was not to try to convert her to my beliefs, she did admit, as time went by, that she was happy for the positive aspects my faith seemed to be affording me. Of course, she also pointed out several areas she thought God had clearly overlooked in my "makeover." And she would say without reserve, "If you didn't have God in your life, Mom, you'd be dead by now." I agree with her on that point! By 1993, my daughter had choreographed her way through a couple of marriages of her own. Still, by her mid-twenties Aimee was a strong young woman with adamant convictions and a sweet, loving heart despite her painful past. I couldn't be more proud of her! For all her efforts, a successful marriage and three beautiful sons were to be in her future.

Still, by the early nineties I wondered at times how God was at work in all that was happening in my life, and I questioned why He hadn't healed my marriage to Richard since we were both believers. At that stage, I continued to try to "analyze" all my painful circumstances and losses. There was no in-depth healing to be had for me at that point because I was still bound by my unforgiveness of myself and others. I didn't know how to spiritually accept God's unconditional love because I felt so unworthy. I hadn't yet learned that I didn't have to earn God's love, it was a free gift—a gift that would take time to fully embrace. Nonetheless, as I look back on those several years after I asked Christ into my life, I see that even though I was disillusioned once again with a failed marriage, the pain of my circumstances didn't own me in quite the way it had before. My depression never took its familiar lethal hold, the acting out of my anger didn't have quite the same depth of drama, and my relationship with my younger son, Cooper, didn't become faint or suffer. Yes, something was undeniably different in me. Although my spiritual transformation waned at times, I was less at the mercy of how I "felt" while being supported with flashes of God's solid truths and protection. No doubt, my guardian angels were working overtime; however, I was still my own worst enemy armed with an unrecognized, unresolved, unforgiven, unhealed past, camouflaged by creative hiding places.

As I was figuring out how to put my arms around my faith, I continued to stumble over my disobedience and propensity to negotiate with God. I thought I trusted that His intentions for me were all for my best, but at that juncture in my life, trust would prove to be elusive. *Submission* was just a word to me then. Yet already woven into the fabric of my heart were God's patient grace and the comfort of the Holy Spirit's voice, which continued to persist over the roar of my soap-operatic circumstances.

New Life in Christ, Old Life on Standby

Early on, my friends, parents, and especially my brother were skeptical of my newfound faith, chalking it up as another one of "Jennifer's missions for fulfillment," which usually took the form of the next husband. I was glommed onto by a Christian and secular "hot news" frenzy and was presented as a potential poster girl of the "born-again-Spirit-filled life." Unfortunately, celebrities are afforded little growing-up time in the Lord because of their public personae. I was asked right off to do the TV talk circuit, which at times turned into a sideshow of sarcastic barbs and Hollywood sympathies. I could almost hear them saying, "Poor thing, there goes another one down the religion drain." Personally, I am not at all religious. I believe that the Bible, Old and New Testaments, is the Word of God, the ultimate truth, authority, and judge of all, inspired by the Holy Spirit. I not only take the Bible to heart, I take it literally. Some trappings of man-made religion are not necessarily based on God's truth. Only God's Word is infallible, not "religion."

During the release of my last book, *People* magazine was doing an article on me and requested photos of Mom, Dad, my husband, Merve, and me for the inside pages. After the shoot, they interviewed my parents, asking them whether they were "born-again Christians" like their daughter. Dad said Rene did the praying for both of them, and Mom quickly responded, "Well, I've always known who Jesus is since I was a baby." Later, I discussed with my parents that everyone has to *ask* Christ into their lives and heart as a personal decision because God gives us free will . . . one does not just inherit salvation. When an individual acknowledges that Jesus Christ is the Son of God, who died for our sins, rose from the grave in three days, and now sits at the right hand of God, then that person is spiritually reborn and eternally saved. "Born again" is not a California cult, nor is it similar to "hitting bottom" and enrolling in the Alcoholics Anonymous program as it is unfortunately so often perceived.

ON FIRE FOR THE LORD

I've been called a lot of things in my life, but never a "shrinking violet." I was on fire on my way to hell, and thank God, I'm now on fire for the Lord! My daughter once said, "Mom, I can't stand that saccharine-sweet Christian 'Oh, I'm so sorry for you, you eternally lost person . . . I'm praying for you!'" True, all too often Christians offer "I'm praying for you" when sometimes they're not. It can sound to unbelievers as if we "Christians" pity their poor little heathen lives. Before I came to the Lord, that's how I would respond if someone said he or she was "praying" for me: My hackles would go up! Sometimes we believers are not terribly tactful about our sincere desire to get God's offer of salvation across to everyone, not just those we personally love. We're not saying that unbelievers are worthless as individuals, we're saying the opposite: God values and loves them so very much, He wants to spend eternity with them!

Now the truth is when we flawed believers acting "in the name of" God mess up, that doesn't mean God is messed up or His offer for eternal life, grace, and forgiveness is flawed. Just because my behavior is less than sterling so much of the time doesn't mean Christ isn't perfect. "Don't kill the message just because the messenger isn't perfect!" It makes me frustrated and, I admit, profoundly sad when God's love flies in the face of closed hearts. Then I'm reminded that I'm not going to enlighten, cajole, or force anyone into salvation. It's the Holy Spirit's job to soften and change hearts; mine is merely to spread the good news of Christ. Still, I do cry for the lost, because I so know how it feels to be nowhere with God, who is everywhere.

NEVER GIVE UP

There are a lot of "closet Christians" in Hollywood because they innately know there exists blackballing and prejudice against professed believers in the entertainment business. It's "in" to be a Scientologist, Buddhist, or New Age guru, but Jesus Christ is definitely "out" (unless of course you are swearing!). In the Word of God, He promises we will suffer for our faith, and that goes double in "Hollywood." Please don't misunderstand me—Tinseltown's turnoff of believers does not compare to the atrocities, deaths, martyrisms, and imprisonments suffered by Christians around the world throughout history as well as today. In this area, thank God, "Hollywood" pales.

In my case, my publicly professed faith was the precursor to a severe drop in employment as I squirmed under scrutiny of public opinion as well as a prejudiced press frothing at the mouth in anticipation of my forecasted fall. I am not a theologian, nor do I profess to be anything more than a tarnished, faulty individual on a journey with the goal of making Christ Lord of my life, and to that end, becoming an effective ambassador of the Holy Spirit. So go ahead and shoot me . . . you won't be the first! Ha!

Detours, crossroads, and obstacles mounted as I headed down my persistent yet shaky path. "I'll never give up," became my new theme. Remember my best friends growing up, me, myself, and I? Well, they were not faring too well in the light of the Father, Son, and Holy Spirit. Sin nature is worse than superglue mixed with tar under your nails. I scrubbed and scrubbed, but I just couldn't seem to get clean enough. I regularly attended church, studied the Word daily, made a pilgrimage to Israel, shot movies such as *Out of Jerusalem—The Book of Acts*, wrote Christian songs, changed some friends and focus, witnessed like crazy to everyone—everywhere—and worked on my relationship with my parents, who had moved in with Coop and me, all the while struggling with my fleet of demons who tempted me at every turn. I definitely wasn't familiar enough then with the armor of God, which enables us to engage prayer and the Holy Spirit as weapons in spiritual warfare. Now I put on my armor every single day!

> Finally, be strong in the Lord and in his mighty power. Put on the full armor of God so that you can take your stand against the devil's schemes. For our struggle is not against flesh and blood, but against the rulers, against the authorities, against the powers of this dark world and against the spiritual forces of evil in the heavenly realms. (Ephesians 6:10–12)

LORD OF MY LIFE

Early on as a Christian, it was wisely suggested to me by my pastor that I lay low with the public proclamation of my faith and take a few years to study the Word and grow in my personal relationship with Christ. I did, and it was the best decision I could have ever made. Accepting the invitation to receive Christ in my life as Savior was a moment of decision founded on faith, but then making God "Lord of my life" became the first step on the road to victory. I already knew feelings were unreliable and would always be changing, but it took substantial time to really believe that God never changes and is always trustworthy. God was showing me unconditional love so that my search for acceptance could finally rest in Him, but I was still so inconsistent. In 1987 I was saved but not yet salvaged. What was I doing wrong?

> That if you confess with your mouth, "Jesus is Lord," and believe in your heart that God raised him from the dead, you will be saved. (Romans 10:9)

The earliest creed or confession of the New Testament church was not "Jesus is Savior" but "Jesus is *Lord*" (Acts 8:16; 19:5; 1 Corinthians 12:3). In the New Testament of the NIV Study Bible, Jesus Christ is specifically called Savior sixteen times, and Lord more than 450 times.

When it occurred to me that "Lord" is proclaimed more times in the Bible than any of the following words: *believer, church, comfort, cross, deliver, eternal, faith, father, good, holy, healed, heart, heaven, justice, life, love, power, prayer, priest, prophet, righteous, shepherd,* and *way* . . . I started to get the message.

When I finally accepted God as Lord of my life, my top priority, source of truth, protector, navigator, disciplinarian, author of love, and ultimate authority, I became His, and my life began to fill with glory, blessings, and miracles!

Today, I feel like a war-horse pulling a wagon full of experiences to share rather than an emotionally needy person on a frantic search for love. Back then, my slow-motion conversion had only struck its first few chords, and learning how to prioritize and move forward to solid ground in my faith at times seemed an insurmountable task. Although the hole in my heart was instantly filled by my answering Jesus' invitation to salvation, there were still some devastating ghosts lingering about from my past. I knew this was not going to be a walk filled with fairy tales and instant gratification. Yet somehow, way down deep in my soul, I also knew I was being watched over by a loving, all-powerful Father who would never let me down. There is a saying in the entertainment business: "Old actors never die; they just fail to perform." Well, not me! Take it from a die-hard overachiever: I was at once saved and forever changing, but not until I gave it all to God did my life really begin to regenerate from the inside out . . . from the power of sin to the power of the Lord. Instead of floundering about amid the cobwebs of my mind, I went to the only ultimately reliable source and found the answers to all my questions in the Word of God. When I took in the Bible on a consistent basis, my life really began to unfold. Yes, there is light at the end of the tunnel, and no, it is not a train. The light is God.

THE KEY TO HAPPINESS

Back then, I was a new person in Christ, but I was still walking around in my old skin, and I still believed somewhere that marriage held the key to my happiness. I wanted a godly companion to share the rest of my life with, and I wasn't willing to wait. I knew that I had fallen sorely short of the mothering mark with my first two children, but I had been able, with the grace of God, to finally begin to be the kind of mom to my last child I had always striven to be. I felt I was ready for a real family and prayed God would allow me one last chance to find happiness as a wife.

Five years into my Christian walk I married yet again. Neil was a believer deepening in his faith, a man who told me that in his heart he wanted to be my "knight in shining armor." That was not to be. The moment Neil confessed that he had failed to tell me something of central importance before we were married, I knew we were doomed. It wasn't because I couldn't understand his withholding the information—I certainly have been caught in a lie or two million in my life. It was really because I had such low tolerance about trust issues that I shut down on him emotionally. Our marriage was annulled.

I was numb and lost when Richard came back into my life as a "friend." Suddenly we were having lunches together, spending hours just talking about everything—our fears, our losses, our faith, our son, our aspirations. We had never been so close. It seemed he had changed somehow. He was gentle and supportive, and I thought that perhaps we were meant to be together after all.

Richard and I remarried, with Cooper present, while I was shooting a film in Mexico. Now Cooper could enjoy the model family he always deserved! I was ecstatic for our son above all else. We moved the entire family (kids, parents, dogs, and horses) to Nashville in hopes of igniting the music career Richard had always dreamed of. As for me, I had several major contracts signed, sealed, and then not delivered that took my finances spiraling down in a deadly confluence of bad timing and bad luck. Bankruptcy loomed again, and I fought it off as I had before by selling everything I owned. I moved out of the Nashville farm into a much smaller place. It was a very scary time—everything was collapsing around me, and it seemed I could not do a thing to stop it. Richard withdrew and his rages began again, bigger and meaner than ever. He moved out, demanding a divorce for the second time. I was about to "go through the fire," not only privately, but publicly. All of my other life experiences were a piece of cake in comparison to the spiritual reshaping looming ahead of me. I hurt; I was stripped of everything . . . it was excruciating.

I believed that God could heal everything, so why wasn't He healing my second marriage to Richard? I fasted, I prayed, I talked to my pastor, I gathered with prayer warriors, I gave Richard space, I cried, I assumed every spiritual position including begging with God to intervene. I couldn't imagine letting Cooper down again. I couldn't imagine my heart being able to take one more failure. Then I went back and begged Richard again; he could pick the counselor, church, believers in accountability, as long as he worked on our marriage and came back home. I found out the hard way—you can't make a meatball bounce, and you can't make someone stay when he's already gone. The only way to make a relationship work is to remain where you are while you work on working it out.

THE CROSSROADS

Not only did Richard refuse to come home or attend church or counseling, he unequivocally wanted a divorce. He said it was over, there was no hope, there was nothing to work on. Richard's demand of divorce was met and reported as front-page newspaper gossip. He had declared our marriage null and void . . . if not forgotten, definitely finished. I hit a crossroads with God that evening. Lost on the highway while driving home after a business meeting, I *really* lost it. I was screaming at God for deserting me and allowing my marriage to fail. I was inconsolable, furious, and irrational. Then I was stopped by a policeman for speeding—which I was. My big, bad attitude bumped into his big, bad attitude and he charged me with a DUI. By the morning news, the wheels of injustice were set in motion. I was squashed between "polite" conversations, accusations, invitations, and gossip. Suddenly I was dealing with a political court battle that remained in the headlines for almost two years. I was finally exonerated by a jury's unanimous "not guilty" . . . but not before my reputation had been slashed and hacked.

More important than any of that was my then-teenager Reis's decline into trouble as a reaction to his father's abandoning him. I managed to put Reis into a "Wilderness Counseling Program," which stabilized him, but when the dust settled, I still found myself at that very serious crossroads with God!

I was brought to my knees; some call it a "spiritual desert." Publicly, I was so blistered, dehydrated, and fried, the only thing I was good for was ongoing "press pickings." Either I was going straight back to my old way of life, or I would have to somehow grow closer to the Lord.

> Godly sorrow brings repentance that leads to salvation and leaves no regret, but worldly sorrow brings death. (2 Corinthians 7:10)

> In this you greatly rejoice, though now for a little while you may have had to suffer grief in all kinds of trials. These have come so that your faith—of greater worth than gold, which perishes even though refined by fire—may be proved genuine and may result in praise, glory and honor when Jesus Christ is revealed. (1 Peter 1:6–7)

I chose Jesus Christ (again!), and this time it felt like a graduation. As I walked into the fire, I was afraid as it engulfed me. I fell on my face, humbled and submissive as the flames licked the air around me. I didn't know what God was going to do with me. It was then that I truly asked for His will, not mine, in my life. It was then that I stopped wailing and moaning, and it was then that God gave me a peace beyond understanding.

Submit yourselves, then, to God. Resist the devil, and he will flee from you. Come near to God and he will come near to you. Wash your hands, you sinners, and purify your hearts, you double-minded. Grieve, mourn and wail. Change your laughter to mourning and your joy to gloom. Humble yourselves before the Lord, and he will lift you up. (James 4:7–10)

I stood and walked out of the fire in victory. I was shaky, but alive in Him. The worldly stakes and attacks escalated higher and higher, but they didn't bury me because my game plan had changed. I had finally given it up to God—not perfectly, just war zone by war zone. No, the details and stresses of my life didn't get easier, they got harder and more threatening. Still, the worse my circumstances became, the more I relied on God, and I finally started to develop that oh-so-sweet, intimate relationship with my Lord that I know now is based on true love and trust. Ever so slowly—my circumstances didn't lead me like a victim to slaughter—truth set me free, and Christ became Lord of my life.

As for my endless quest for love and marriage? I met Mervin Louque when I first moved to Nashville. We were working together on an on-line project and were introduced to each other by a mutual friend. Our first round was all business, but after a year of working together, things between us took on a different complexion—we fell in love. Mervin and I just celebrated our fifth anniversary (and they said it wouldn't last!).

There is so much I have learned from the Lord about marriage and relationships, but the most striking notion is the reality of giving it up and getting it back. And remember, I am the expert in all these things . . . because I've done everything wrong! And on top of that, at age fifty-three, smack-dab in the middle of menopause, with a fourteen-year-old at home and a relatively new marriage, I often remind any who may cross my path that a woman in menopause is like a Doberman with lipstick . . . "Don't mess with me, you'll lose." (I am still working very hard on my "quiet, gentle spirit"—I promise, Lord.)

When ladies my age gather in a room and someone says, "Is it hot in here or is it me?" we'll respond with knowing empathy, "It's you, Hot Flash!" Shared experiences and commonality can ease life's discomforts. "At least I'm not the only one!" is our cry of relief. If there was any relief to your night sweats other than setting the air conditioner at arctic temperatures (so that your husband has to wear a winter coat and mittens to bed for the next five years!), wouldn't you share the good news with your fellow sufferers? Not all areas that "ail" us are experienced dur- ing a "season." Some can haunt and rob us for our entire lives like an incurable disease left undetected. Personally, I was sick and tired of being emotionally and spiritually sick and tired, and I asked God to show me how to be free. And with that I was on to my next mission . . . with a vengeance.

FOOTSTEPS

Your promised love
Stayed by my side
I'd find Your footsteps in the sand—
Next to mine

But when I was older
Fears looking over my shoulder
I couldn't find
Your footsteps in the sand
Next to mine

And in my worst of times
I felt so alone
Just a game darkness played on me
But now I see
That You were carrying me
Carrying me home—when I was tired

You healed the little girl in me
Set my soul free
I'll always find
Your footsteps in the sand
Next to mine

WORDS AND MUSIC BY JENNIFER O'NEILL.
HANDSHAKE PRODUCTIONS.
USED BY PERMISSION.

3

Echoes of My Heart

The Search for God's Love

Am I weak in the knees in love or just arthritic?
–J. O'N

ASK A CHILD TO CHOOSE BETWEEN A NICKEL AND a dime, and he'll take the nickel every time because the nickel looks bigger. I chased nickels for years. Immediate gratification versus eternal treasures—sometimes it takes forever to learn the value of the latter. For those of us who have asked for God's lordship and blessings in life despite the bruises we sport, we're graciously protected, loved, forgiven, and saved in Christ—the true eternal treasure.

It's hard to miss something we've never known. Do we yearn for things we've never had, seen, felt, touched, tasted, or experienced? Is ignorance really bliss?

As a young girl, the "hole in my heart" evolved slowly until I ached to the point of feeling empty. Something just didn't seem right, and it made me sad and frightened to my core. I couldn't put my finger on this emptiness; I couldn't explain it then, but I felt I was slowly slipping away. It seemed a step beyond the lack of affirmation from my parents or the feeling of being invisible. I thought I had to fight for this elusive "filling." Maybe I could earn it? Please, someone give it to me! Obviously, I didn't know that God was "It." Then, all I knew for sure was that I'd never make it without "it"—whatever "it" was—and without "it," I was worthless. I thought of myself as merely someone else's reflection. It didn't occur to me that the individual source of my mirrored reflection could be just as cracked and distorted as my reflected self-image. I was bound by a worldly standard run by fallen, self-centered people, myself being one.

SELF-ESTEEM

You've heard it said, "The opposite of love is not hate, it is indifference." Parents are their children's first caretakers of esteem, godly direction, and affirmation. But we can't give what we haven't received, and so many parents are themselves damaged little boys and girls who need healing in their own hearts before they can pass on real love to their kids. I know; I was that kind of absentee parent to two of my three children. I've apologized profusely to my older two, Aimee and Reis, for not being there for them as every child deserves a parent to be. The truth is, I had them before I had me . . . and that's never a pretty picture. Just as with my parents, it wasn't malicious on my part.

The saying "The apple doesn't fall far from the tree" is true, but that fact doesn't have to plague our lineage. Breaking the pattern of generational sin is possible. We must first recognize our hurts from the root of the pain. I have to regularly ask myself, Do these responses, feelings, and acting out of those feelings, live in my now or in my past? Acknowledging our pain is the first step toward desiring healing in our lives. Is anything here familiar?

LOW SELF-ESTEEM FEELINGS

Invisible	Unheard
Unlovable	Unaffirmed
Rejected	Criticized
Shamed	Devalued

RESULTING FEELINGS

Anger	Anxiety
Depression	Disappointment
Sadness	Loneliness
Hopelessness	Fearfulness
Frustration	Frantic
Bitterness	Guilt
Envy	Self-doubt
Self-hatred	

ACTING OUT OF THOSE FEELINGS

Addictive behaviors	Suicidal thoughts
Eating disorders	Destructive relationships
Antisocial behavior	Promiscuity
Mental and physical illnesses	

I'm well aware of where my low self-esteem originated. This is not a finger-pointing mission, just some background. (Remember, "If you throw dirt, you lose ground"—I was going to write a country song with that title!) But it is so important to recognize, understand, and grieve the original pain so that forgiveness and healing can occur. Let's look at our personal pasts—all the parts we can remember and own. Please know that there may be a boatload of details pushed so far back in our hearts and minds that they elude our memories right now, but later on we will step through all this and more with the power and direction of the Holy Spirit. Not a single one of the enemy's dark footholds can survive the light of truth and God's absolute power of forgiveness and healing! Don't worry, this is a time to be excited! Do your best to honestly identify personal areas of behavioral responses to pain—pain that you experienced but did not necessarily author. What you did with that pain was your first step of personal responsibility. Of course we didn't know what else to do with all our hurts, but soon we'll acknowledge that recognition allows healing, while denial imprisons. Each of us has our own recipe of reactions to pain, hurt, and anger as well as unique expressions of acting out our low self-esteem issues and responses. All the steps of our manifested pain are traceable, forgivable, and healable with God's power and love. But you have to do your part!

It is crucial to recognize the self-centered, selfish personality traits that leech onto those of us suffering from low self-esteem. Prior to forgiveness and healing, we'll inevitably insist that the world revolve around our pain as we find negative ways to demand what we consider to be our rightful affirmation from others. The enemy loves this tool of destruction!

SIN NATURE

We all have "sin nature." We were born with it, and cannot overcome it by our own might, good deeds, or heroic desires. Because of it, we suffer at our own hands in addition to the pain inflicted on us from outside forces. Believe me, I'm not making light of the deep wounds caused by others on so many innocent hearts, but regardless of the offense, ours or theirs, our past does not have to own our present or our future. God has promised us that!

> Brothers, I do not consider myself yet to have taken hold of it. But one thing I do: Forgetting what is behind and straining toward what is ahead, I press on toward the goal to win the prize for which God has called me heavenward in Christ Jesus. (Philippians 3:13–14)

As far as our sin nature goes, I've told God that I didn't like inheriting such an ugly thing! Why do we all have it? The answer is simple: "generational sin." God drove home the point with an illustration: I had an occasion to visit a roomful of two- and three-year-old toddlers. The babies were so cute and roly-poly! I love babies and never can get enough of them, so when I walked into this room, I felt as if I was in heaven. That was until I noticed their behavior; they were bashing each other over the head and poking each other in the eyes. The big ones were pulling the toys away and pushing the little ones over, oblivious to their tears. In short, they were little self-centered brats on their way to growing into big self-centered brats. That's human nature. And while all of that was going on, the mothers were saying, "Be nice" . . . "Say please" . . . "Say thank you" . . . "Don't do that; that's not nice." What has become very clear to me is that we can learn manners, but we can't be transformed without Christ.

The *recognition* of our sin nature and need for healing is the first step to freedom. Complacency is Satan's waterbed that lulls us to sleep in mediocrity. The enemy loves halfhearted efforts and numbed responses that lead to unfulfilled dreams and broken families. Those who are lazy, mean, and critical, and who exhibit self-centered, godless behavior lead the enemy's top-ten list of trophies. Are you a stuffed head on his mantel? I sure was!

Start now by acknowledging, even claiming, the negative feelings and behaviors in your life. Look at the list and put a name and a face to each one . . . yours! Don't fall into the trap of denial, with a merry "That's someone else, not me." Remember, now is the time to just "flag" your areas of need. Slaying the dragons comes later. Here's a constant reminder for you that I will repeat ad nauseam: *You are not alone!* God will never desert you as you work your way toward Him and toward your healing.

> I, even I, am he who blots out your transgressions, for my own sake, and remembers your sins no more. (Isaiah 43:25)

When I realized that I was reconciled to God through His Son's ultimate sacrifice and that God does not even *remember* my sins, I wept, crawled across the pages of my past, praised, prayed, and genuflected in my heartfelt desire just to be obedient. I knew I couldn't be perfect, but I could strive to be as obedient as I possibly could. Just like Paul, though, sometimes when I want to do something, I find myself doing the exact opposite.

> I do not understand what I do. For what I want to do I do not do, but what I hate I do. And if I do what I do not want to do, I agree that the law is good. As it is, it is no longer I myself who do it, but it is sin living in me. I know that nothing good lives in me, that is, in my sinful nature. For I have the desire to do what is good, but I cannot carry it out. For what I do is not the good

I want to do; no, the evil I do not want to do—this I keep on doing. (Romans 7:15–19)

I recognized my need to be healed because my life was bound by my unresolved past. I lived that fact out daily through my addictions, anger, sadness, and distancing of myself from God and others. I didn't have God's peace or know His design for me because I hadn't forgiven. Unforgiveness will stop a believer cold.

FORGIVING MYSELF AND OTHERS

It has been only recently that I have asked and then allowed the Holy Spirit to shepherd me through the process of *revealing, forgiving, then receiving forgiveness, confessing, repenting, and healing.* Just as fifteen years ago I had to *ask* Christ into my heart before I received salvation, I also had to ask God to truly heal me through the power of the Holy Spirit. Healing is not an automatic process that comes with grace; it is only released by and with a sincere request! I finally prayed that the Holy Spirit would show me all my hidden, dark places and vulnerable creases of old pain, bringing my secrets and conveniently forgotten sins to light so I could be healed. Before I accepted Christ as Lord of my life, I was doomed to suffer the enemy's crippling emotional thievery fueled by my unresolved past and unforgiveness. My promised victory did not come instantly as a free pass with my salvation; it was a process, and will remain an ongoing, lifelong process. To realize we are ultimately responsible for everything we think, say, and do is an extremely sobering truth once finally and fully owned.

Each of us has his or her own story, and I pray our choices lead us to God's grand, individual plan for our lives. I have found, however, that this will not happen without a clean slate of forgiveness and healing, and a keen ear to hear the whisperings of the Holy Spirit. This is our passport to our complete potential in Him. The combination to the lock that held me back from God's fullness after accepting Christ was not a secret or an unsolved mystery. It was not some frustrating hit-or-miss lottery. It was not about being smart or wearing the right clothes. In His Word, God tells us everything we'll ever need to know about everyone, everything, and every circumstance, including exactly how He will heal us.

In Matthew 6:9–15, Jesus tells us how to pray:

> Our Father in heaven,
> hallowed be your name,
> your kingdom come,
> your will be done
>   on earth as it is in heaven.
> Give us today our daily bread.
> Forgive us our debts,
>   as we also have forgiven our debtors.
> And lead us not into temptation,
> but deliver us from the evil one.
>
> For if you forgive men when they sin against
> you, your heavenly Father will also forgive you.
> But if you do not forgive men their sins, your
> Father will not forgive your sins.

There it is, as clear as the nose on my face! Even as we Christians pray the Lord's Prayer, we end it before the last two verses, no matter what translation of the Bible we're using. Don't ignore those last two verses. Heed God's reiteration of the importance of *our* forgiveness as it relates to our *being forgiven.* Herein lies the rub, God's first commandment:

> Love the LORD your God with all your heart and with all your soul and with all your strength. (Deuteronomy 6:5)

and

> . . . love your neighbor as yourself. (Leviticus 19:18)

In the New Testament, Jesus says,

> "Love the Lord your God with all your heart and with all your soul and with all your mind. This is the first and greatest commandment." And the second is like it: "Love your neighbor as yourself." (Matthew 22:37–39)

Please remember, God never asks us to do anything that He does not empower us to fulfill through the Holy spirit. Also, if you love someone, you do not hold that person in unforgiveness. Moreover, God commands us to forgive everyone of everything (even ones we do not hold in love!). Forgiveness does not mean we have to "do business again" with those who hurt us. It just means our unforgiveness won't rob us of our healing, happiness, and peace! It does not mean we condone or disregard our offender's actions against us; we just choose to release him or her of our unforgiveness and give all our pain back to Christ, leaving all retribution to God.

If, for example, you find yourself in the excruciating pain of a broken marriage and must forgive your ex-husband for his offenses against you (just as he must forgive you if he is to be healed), you also know you would not want another dose of that person. Yet, if you have children with him, you *do* have to "do business with him again" in respect to, and for the sake of, your kids. If your ex-husband's behavior remains hurtful and damaging, and through the power of the Holy Spirit you have forgiven him, you must allow God's spiritual protection and discernment to shield you from whatever form the offender's ongoing fiery arrows may take. Ask God to give you that supernatural Teflon coating called "choice." You can *choose* not to let his attacks affect you negatively! You can *choose* to rise above even the most premeditated onslaughts, praying for your ex-husband and loving him as Christ would, but hating and rebuking his sin so that it doesn't have entry into your heart. With every sunset, nighttime declares the "fading day" part of our most recent past. Just as God instructs us not to let the sun go down on our anger lest it turn to sin, He also tells us to deal with our unforgiveness on a daily basis.

GIVE THE PAIN TO JESUS

Even if you have healed after forgiveness, it doesn't mean the memory of the pain doesn't still affect or offend you. It just doesn't own you. Remind yourself that you have given those places and areas of hurt back to Jesus. In doing so you let *Him* deal with your offender. Remember, you are no longer the debtholder. This, of course, applies to everyone you are required to keep dealing with in your life—bosses, children, family members, authority figures, etc.

> Do not take revenge, my friends, but leave room for God's wrath,
> for it is written: "It is mine to avenge; I will repay," says the Lord.
> (Romans 12:19)

Forgiveness leading to healing is not instant whiteout! If you turn off your emotions like a water tap, you're not healed, you're numb. We're not supposed to stop feeling; we're supposed to stop dealing out paybacks. Yes, there is righteous indignation (Jesus in the Temple), but remember, we are not to take the law into our own hands. We're supposed to rest in our Lord Jesus' protection in the knowledge that He died for all *our* sin. It's so easy to forgive once we truly digest what *we* have been forgiven of in Christ. If we hold on to our unforgiveness, we are in essence telling God, "Thanks for the offer of the blood of Your only begotten Son for my sake, but I think I'll hold on to my anger and hurt anyway." God's design for our salvation and spiritual well-being is perfect . . . even if we don't understand it. We don't have to do anything but be obedient, and God will do the rest. It begins with submitting to the Lord so He can do His work in us and through us! Please reread these two Scriptures:

> Submit yourselves, then, to God. Resist the devil, and he will flee from you. Come near to God and he will come near to you. Wash your hands, you sinners, and purify your hearts, you double-minded. Grieve, mourn and wail. Change your laughter to mourning and your joy to gloom. Humble yourselves before the Lord, and he will lift you up. (James 4:7–10)

> Be kind and compassionate to one another, forgiving each other, just as in Christ God forgave you. (Ephesians 4:32)

When we receive our healing through our forgiveness, we need to write down every area we traveled and reexperienced with the Holy Spirit—areas we then gave back to Jesus. Our healing needs to be reclaimed *every day* because every part of us, as a spiritual work in progress, needs daily maintenance, encouragement, confirmation, repentance, covering, forgiveness, and healing. Then we can rejoice and enjoy every moment God graces us with.

THE HARDEST PART

We are not to hold *ourselves* in unforgiveness no matter what our indiscretions. Jesus has already paid the price on the cross. Yet I often find forgiving myself is the part that feels so impossible! God knows this and never asks anything of us that we cannot achieve through the power of His Holy Spirit. Remember, while on this earth, Jesus did not do one thing without the power of prayer. What a relief, since left to my own devices, I'm about as effective as an umbrella in a hurricane.

I love the way God speaks to us through real people in the Bible with real problems and shortcomings. People like Noah, Moses, Solomon, David, and Peter are our mentors, teachers, and disciples of His love. Flawed and foolish, the Biblical scribes, led by the Holy Spirit, tell us unequivocally what God wants us to know about every possible circumstance of life and beyond. They do this sandwiched between their personal insecurities, fallen natures, and sinful side steps. They are arrogant, insecure, lustful, murdering, adulterous, drunken, shameless, lying, turncoat, fallen examples of humanity who love the Lord with all their hearts and sincerely confess, repent, forgive, and claim victory and wholeness and healing through God's forgiveness.

Very soon after I accepted Christ in my life, every part of me was convicted by my repeated mistakes. I wanted to be so good, but so much of the time I felt so bad. This was a result of my "overachieving"—thinking I could earn love while ignoring God's free gift of grace. To put it simply, it took me a very long time to realize that my best intentions were usually different from God's best for me. His way is the highway to happiness, and the only detours along the way are due to my reconstruction, not a bend in His road. The map is clear. God is on our side, so if I'm confused or lost, I need to stop and wait on Him, ask His direction, and follow His leading precisely. I find whenever I do that, I'm "home," no matter where I happen to be. And, I finally have a whole heart, not a hole in my heart!

FATHER IN HEAVEN

You were my weekend father, since I was ten
Nothing much felt right after then
Mom said you loved me, Mom said you'd be by
But when you left for good, you had tears in your eyes

Father in Heaven, bring my dad home
It's not right, your children are alone

Mom went to work, to put food on the shelf
She said, call the neighbors if you need any help
I got in some trouble, oh, I made some mistakes
I started to do whatever it takes

Father in Heaven, bring my mom home
It's not right, your children are alone

Now I talk to my Father who lives in the sky
His Holy Spirit's in me, His Son never lies
I know He loves my mom and dad
Even though they couldn't stay
He loves us all, even when we turn away

I had this place, deep in my heart
Never satisfied, it was tearing me apart
But Father God, He never lets me down
I was lost, now I'm found

Father in Heaven bring love to our home
Without it, our children are alone
Father in Heaven, make Your presence known
In Your arms, Your children are never alone

WORDS AND MUSIC BY JENNIFER O'NEILL.
HANDSHAKE PRODUCTIONS.
USED BY PERMISSION.

4

Someone Else's Mirror

Discovering the Beauty Within

*Patience is found when I put myself
at the back of the line.*
—J. O'N

WE WERE RUNNING LATE AS MOM HERDED MY
brother and me down the sidewalk toward our destination in
mid-Manhattan. Next to us was a building under construction
surrounded by a chain-link fence that guarded the machinery.
That's when Mom tripped and began her amazing voyage from
one end of the block to the other. Mike and I stood frozen as the
hurried New Yorkers on lunch break who packed the sidewalk
parted like the Red Sea, allowing Mom a wide berth. You would
have thought you were watching a stumbling drunk, but in fact,
Mom was just a victim of a string of bad luck. It was an amazing sight, and as usually happens in moments like that, my perspective was in slow motion.

Her little stumble was nothing to write home about, but it set
off a sequence of events that sent Mom headfirst into the chain-
link fence, which in turn slingshotted her back into the sea of
pedestrians with amazing accuracy and lack of grace. If fate had
smiled on her, she would have fallen then and there and been done

with it. But no, instead, she ricocheted off a lamppost, and in a herculean attempt to regain her composure, fell into a Fred Astaire side step that landed her, yet again, face-to-fence with the construction site. Some people who attempted to grab her in assistance missed; others watched in total amazement, silently placing bets on her outcome. Many, I'm sure, pitied Mike and me as poor abused children with a lush for a parent. Mom bounced, twirled, and careened all the way to the next curb where the battle finally ended as she crashed to her knees in the gutter. The instant she fell, all motion returned to normal speed and reality presented itself in the form of two huge gaping holes in Mom's stockings. Other than that, she was "fine," or at least that's what she kept saying to the masses that gathered about her in curiosity.

NEVER GOOD ENOUGH

Have you ever felt as though you've fallen flat on your face with the whole world watching? I've spent most of my life trying to recover from my own falls—and all of that time I've wanted desperately to live in someone else's mirror. Even though I've been in the "beauty business" for decades and been considered a success in front of the camera, I was still caught in the trap of low self-esteem with its ever-present sidekick, "Never good enough." These destructive voices escorted me through years of painful competition with myself and others.

When I was a girl, the perfect female picture was framed as Veronica in the *Archie* comic books. A two-inch waist, long, shapely legs, an hourglass figure, and cascading thick hair were the set standard for preteen girls. Even Annette Funicello graduated from being a mouse into a bathing suit queen stirring up hormones with the *Beach Blanket Bingo* set. Who could compete?

Our own daughters continue to carry the banner of striving for the cover-girl look with bouts of bulimia and skewed perceptions of perfection shoved down their throats with every fashion statement, new "star," and turn of the magazine page. A recent *USA Today* article stated that 80 percent of preteen girls today are either on a diet or thinking about their weight, one unhealthy way or another.

The dichotomy for me was that, although I was on magazine covers from the time I was fifteen, I was still that insecure, damaged little girl. When I have the opportunity to speak to thousands of women at a time, the pain I see in so many of their eyes reflects the anger and choking feelings of not being good enough, pretty enough, or loved enough. It just breaks my heart because I personally know how deep those feelings run, and how powerfully our negative tapes can reinforce our fears if allowed to run our lives. I also know that being a "cover girl" doesn't automatically get you the gold in the self-esteem olympics.

As a working model I had the reputation of being aloof and cold. I was neither. In reality, I was painfully shy and uncomfortable in my own skin. Although it was excruciating to feel that way for the most part, I do remember one incident that makes me giggle to this day. I've always had very small feet for my five-foot-eight-inch frame. I used to wear size five and a half to six shoes, whereas most models stepped along in boat sizes of nine or ten. I would describe my feet as Flintstone-shaped—with squared-off toes, but they're still dainty and supported by good arches. Truth be known, I'm sure the models secretly envied me—there's nothing terribly feminine about having pontoons for feet!

I was on a location shoot with five other models for *Harper's Bazaar* magazine. The editor was assigning clothes and accessories—hats, jewelry, and open sandals were still left to photograph. I honestly thought the editor pointed at me to get a pedicure as the sandal model . . . silly me. When I took off my shoes to have my toes polished, the editor laughed viciously, directing all the models' attention to my small, square feet. Then, in a belittling whine she said, "Jennifer, how could you even think I would feature such ridiculous excuses for feet in my magazine?" I shrank into the corner in red-faced embarrassment. What really hurt was that the one feature of my anatomy I was proud of had suddenly become an embarrassment. In my shame, it took a while for me to notice that the editor wore size eleven shoes. I eventually chalked up the whole incident to jealousy on her part. I reclaimed my feet as "small" pluses, no matter what she or anyone else thought. Unfortunately, I did not fare as well in other areas of insecurity that held me hostage well into adulthood. Self-criticism and self-loathing often turn emotionally needy, self-centered little girls into emotionally needy, self-centered women who are clueless as to what it feels like to live up to God's description of our feminine potential:

A wife of noble character who can find? She is worth far more than rubies. Her husband has full confidence in her and lacks nothing of value. She brings him good, not harm, all the days of her life . . . She is clothed with strength and dignity; she can laugh at the days to come. She speaks with wisdom, and faithful instruction is on her tongue. She watches over the affairs of her household and does not eat the bread of idleness. Her children arise and call her blessed; her husband also, and he praises her: "Many women do noble things, but you surpass them all." Charm is deceptive, and beauty is fleeting; but a woman who fears the LORD is to be praised. (Proverbs 31:10–12, 25–30)

Wow, what an honorable goal to shoot for. Better than that, God says that we each can become that woman if we unleash the power of the Holy Spirit in us! I decided to "sign up" to do just that.

RECOGNIZING GOD'S EXTRAVAGANT LOVE

Where does the enemy live? In hopelessness. I have been there—clinically depressed and hospitalized to undergo shock therapy, analyzed and homogenized beyond recognition. The lows of life experienced in the dark can be downright deadly. After spending years in therapy, I could analyze my pain, its origins, and its tendencies, but I was never healed in the process. I was never able to connect my head with my heart until I accepted Christ as my Savior. Even after I received my faith, my healings were inconsistent until I made Christ the *Lord of my life.* Further, my healings were incomplete until I truly *forgave out of obedience.* Along the way I tortured myself about how I was to become a reliable mother, wife, friend, and Christian. The answer was, certainly not by my own power, but by His—and by *focusing!* It's hard for us and our families not to get waylaid in the world jungle:

- The American Academy of Pediatrics reports that the average eighteen-year-old has viewed about two hundred thousand acts of violence on television alone.

- The Centers for Disease Control reports that even though teen birth rates during 1991–96 declined for all racial and ethnic groups, about one million teenagers become pregnant each year; 95 percent of those pregnancies are unintended, and almost one-third end in abortion. (There were 1.3 million *reported* abortions in the U.S. during 1992–96 [*The World Almanac and Book of Facts,* 2001].)

- According to the Bureau of the Census, in 1998, of the 103 million households in the United States, only 36 percent could be considered "traditional" households, i.e., consisting of a married couple with one or more children.

- Latest statistics show 1.4 million incidences of violent crime during 1999 alone (*The World Almanac and Book of Facts,* 2001).

Evil is everywhere, as evidenced by the rampant suicide rate of our teenagers. We know it's a mess out there, but how do we elude the garbage bin?

SAVING GRACE

For me, staying on track was tough because in the beginning I was certain God wouldn't have time for me, let alone love me, warts and all. When I first came to Christ, I was working with a Christian counselor on what was for me a revolutionary new concept—grace. This was not *earning* God's love and protection, but *asking for,* and then *accepting,* His free gift. During a long session, I broke down and wept, "I don't think He has time for me. God is a busy guy!" Of course, that feeling came from growing up with parents that didn't seem to have time for me, so I concluded that my Father in heaven couldn't possibly have personal attention for pathetic old me either.

My counselor smiled knowingly. "How many children do you have?" At the time I had two. She continued softly, "What did you feel when you had your first child?"

I thought for a moment. "When I had Aimee, I felt I could never love anyone or anything more in the whole world."

"What about your second child?" she countered.

It didn't take me long to get the point. A new song stirred in my heart: "You can run out of time, you can run out of money, you can run out of things to say . . . but you can never run out of love!" With that truth came a seed that grew into a hope, and that hope turned me from darkness to light. The shadowed areas of my soul slowly receded into my past where they belonged. I was on my way.

> *Peace* comes when we let go . . .
> *Trust* comes when we believe . . .
> *True love* is always free . . .
> *Faith* is something we can't see.

It takes me to my knees when I think about the fact that less than 20 percent of individuals who reach the age of twenty without receiving salvation ever do accept the saving grace of Jesus Christ. What about us late starters in faith who have lived lives out in the world without God's anchor or covering? For that matter, what about those who have been either closet Christians, mere Sunday attendees, or forlorn followers who are so off the walk, they're stuck in a ditch somewhere beside the beaten path? What about trusting and opening up? When I wrote *Surviving Myself,* I'd never been more afraid in my whole life. Do you know what it's like to create a permanent record of what an idiot you are? I'm not a stupid person, but I've made a lifetime's worth of outrageous mistakes. Yet God was very gracious to me. I remember thinking, *Oh Lord, I can't talk about that! What are people going to think? What are they going to say about me?* Who cares! God reminded me that the truth shall make you free, and I believed that—if I could only get out of my own way!

Shortly after my autobiography had been released, I was booked to speak at the National Prayer Breakfast. I am always so excited to give my testimony to anyone at any time, so I especially looked forward to sharing it with such company as would be present at this prestigious Washington event. That joy was short-lived. I began to feel totally insecure, unworthy, and unprepared as an ambassador for Christ. (This, by the way, is exactly how the enemy tries to derail our efforts.) I was shaking in my boots with one hand on the phone ready to cancel my speech.

Having just moved to a new neighborhood, my husband, Merve, and I had been visiting local churches in hopes of finding one to attend regularly. I had been on my face praying for God to shore up my spiritual underpinnings, especially with the invitation to speak in Washington close at hand. Frankly, I spent so much time genuflecting, I looked like a pancake with feet. As always, if we have our eyes to the heavens and our ears open to the romancing of the Holy Spirit, God's editing of people, places, messages, and events is never less than awe-inspiring. So it was the day we attended the Word of Life Church pastored by Doug Noland. It was an unlikely gathering for us in terms of location, attendees, and style, but Pastor Noland's message was powerfully insightful, and of course, fashioned expressly for my personal edification. Isn't it amazing how hundreds of strangers can attend a single sermon and it seems the Word fits each individual to a tee? His sermon that day was titled "Postcards from Hell"—a look at the enemy's negative messages that feature our failed past as an inevitable rerun for our future. The pastor's sermon was just the message of encouragement I needed. I put my fears on the back burner and placed my trust in God. As always, He was faithful. My Washington speech went swimmingly (for a novice).

THE KEYS TO THE KINGDOM

I will give you the keys of the kingdom of heaven; whatever you
bind on earth will be bound in heaven, and whatever you loose
on earth will be loosed in heaven. (Matthew 16:19)

Yes, Jesus has given us the keys to the Kingdom, that we might
experience victorious living on a daily basis. God also tells us that
making a real difference with our lives for the kingdom begins by
fervently asking for what we desire. For me personally it has been
so disappointing to watch how the enormous potential for
Christian outreach remains virtually untouched in the entertainment field. Someone once challenged me with his belief that if
Christ were on the earth today He'd be in Hollywood, making
movies. It is an interesting concept because the entertainment
business is so powerful by nature of its impact and scope. I can't
help my feeling of annoyance that every Christian movie or project seems doomed by its "dollar-ninety-eight" budget and vision.
I sit on the board of Media Fellowship, a worldwide ministry for
support of Christians in front of, and behind, the camera.
Members include everyone from news anchors to stunt men, pro-
ducers, studio heads, editors, writers, and actors. We are all
intent on creating and distributing entertainment product that is
topnotch as well as compelling. At the same time, we seem to
always be forced to work within a tiny budget. What's wrong
with this picture . . . literally? God doesn't want His children on
tiny budgets, personally, creatively, or businesswise. God wants
us to be spiritually prosperous, generous, strong, and healed!
Remember, "The one who is in you is greater than the one who
is in the world" (1 John 4:4) is not an ad campaign; it's the Word
of God. The people who run Hollywood, for the most part, have

the almighty dollar sitting on their throne. If we the public make it known that we want better entertainment with values and inspirational messages, that is what Hollywood will produce. We're the consumer, after all.

The film industry is called the "2 percent business" of entertainment. This refers to the fact that out of the hundreds of thousands of actors accepted as members in the Screen Actors Guild of America (which, by the way, represents only a small portion of those actors who long to join), only 2 percent make over $7,500 a year. Two percent! Talk about slim-to-none odds.

That was my world, a hugely competitive one, but competition never really scared me, Hollywood or otherwise. Competing on my horses, for example, has always been an exhilarating mixture of anticipation and self-defense. After breaking my neck, back, leg, arm, and ribs on my horses, my theme song became, "Flying through the air with, *hopefully*, the greatest of ease." I vigorously went for top billing in all areas of my life, battling my insecurities along the way. Odd combo, wouldn't you say? Well, maybe not. It was just my way of handling my fears—jump in and swim like a mad woman. One thing for sure, I had a thick enough skin to survive in the business I chose for my vocation. If you sell vacuum cleaners door-to-door and a potential client slams the door in your face, you can always walk away and say, "They didn't like my vacuum cleaners." However, when you're selling *yourself*, your heart, creativity, looks, and talent, the "door slam" can feel like a lethal injection. Amazingly, my career never owned that part of me. Where I became the emergency patient was in my need for affirmation through relationships. If my life were to be measured by the pictures on my piano: friends, family, kids, "loving husband with his protective arm around his sweet wife," then something was painfully amiss. I was the absentee photo lost in my last move from bad decisions to worse choices. My image looked like broken pieces of a shattered mirror with no hope for repair. Before I came to Christ, I would say, "Connect my physical and emotional scars, and what you have is a road map to nowhere." It didn't matter that I was getting top billing on the marquee. Eventually the revelation that "familiar is not necessarily better" began to sink in, and I started moving up the road to recovery, slowly but surely.

UNIVERSAL ISSUES

Recently I spoke to high-school girls, grades eight through twelve, along with some of their moms. In secular schools I am bound by law to state my testimony without including any kind of reference to "religion." Still our Constitution allows me to tell my life story and personal experiences to the kids, so with a lot of sentences beginning with "This is what happened to me," I was able to declare my transformation through Christ. That way God's message is never watered down or lost in the translation! This particular night I touched on personal as well as universal issues with the girls and their moms. We found common ground, unraveling some little-traveled areas of painful emotions. After a delightful hour-plus of drawing the connection between details of my life and theirs, we all laughed, took pictures, and acknowledged some of the forgiveness and healing that, as a whole, needed to be addressed. We tackled every area, from teen suicide, improved parenting, abstinence, peer pressure, abortion, generational sin nature, love, friendship, anger, boundaries, and support systems, as well as a myriad of ways to better deal with our collective needs. It was, as always, an amazing experience of serendipitous blessings from our Father's heavenly helping hand. Believe me, I always get so much more out of these meetings than anyone, and this particular evening was no exception.

One of the girls attending the talk pulled me aside after the "photo-ops" with the others and asked if we could have some private time. My heart raced, praying for the right words and demeanor to present to this one so obviously hurting. For more than forty-five minutes we talked, paced, cried, and hugged beneath the spill of unfriendly fluorescent lights and intermittent passing students headed to their cars. I knew in my heart that this girl's cry for help was a divine appointment, and yet, when I had to leave at the prompting of the security guards, I left the meeting with a sense of ambiguity as well as a dawning clarity: You can't help someone who doesn't choose to help herself. Yes, she had called me out to the hall for some personal time and support, but in the end, she panicked and withdrew in fear. This seventeen-year-old said she had been sexually abused most of her life. She had never told anyone. She had tried to kill herself multiple times and had been hospitalized. She was scared to death and suicidal, but she wouldn't let me get her any help. Believe me, I knew how scary her world could be, especially without Christ in her life, as was my case at her age. I can clearly remember how lost, frantic, and angry I was when no one heard my cries of pain and abandonment. Fast-forward thirty-nine years, and there I was with this little girl, this bundle of raw nerves telling me her life story, then tying my hands by not allowing me to get her some local counseling. I knew I couldn't do the job of helping her long-distance, and I was leaving town the next morning.

What was particularly frustrating was that the therapist I had in mind to help her just happened to come with me to the event. Her name is Bonnie, and I know her to be a solid woman of God as well as a gifted certified Christian counselor. I was able, through the power of the Holy Spirit, to convince the girl to meet that night with Bonnie, and afterwards we both gave the teen our personal numbers so she could reach us anytime. Nonetheless, weeks passed, and neither Bonnie nor I heard from the young lady. Her high school was put on alert, but since she had already been protected from any possible ongoing abuse by moving in with guardians, the agony and pain she was feeling were her choice to address. I pleaded with her to consult with a qualified person about her problems because I knew that she would not be able to deal with such issues on her own. I also told her repeatedly that she was loved, valued, and there was healing for her, but unortunately the demons of depression, anger, and fear held her at bay. I felt as though I was looking into the mirror of my past.

YOU ARE SPECIAL

If we do not choose Jesus, we will not be saved; and God says that every level of our salvation, transfiguration, regeneration, sanctification, forgiveness, and healing is a direct answer to our prayer requests. We must *ask* to *receive;* there is no other way. Yes, we are worthy to our Lord. Remember, He died for us!

Just in case you're not feeling very special to yourself or anyone else lately, please read this love letter, then have a short cry, take a deep breath, and know how adored you really are in God's eyes.

My Love,

Please accept this extravagant gift of life that I'm offering you (Romans 5:17–21). Come to Me and you will find that I am gentle and humble (Matthew 11:29). I am merciful, slow to anger, and full of grace (Psalm 145:8). My heart beats wildly every time you look My direction (Solomon 4:9). Follow Me and

I will give you the desires of your heart (Psalm 37:4) because I am passionately in love with you (Psalm 45:11).

Nothing, absolutely nothing can change My love for you (Romans 8:38–39). Trust in Me and I will help you (Romans 10:11). I'll welcome you with open arms (Mark 10:16), and I will meet all of your needs (Philippians 4:19). I will love you all day and sing songs to you at night (Psalm 42:8). You mean the world to Me, and My love for you knows no limits (John 3:16).

Let Me live in your heart and I'll breathe new life into you (Romans 8:11). Just invite Me in and all of heaven will celebrate (Luke 15:7). I'll be with you every day of your life (Matthew 28:20) and fill you with hope (Romans 15:13) because you belong to Me. You are Mine (Exodus 19:5). I gave up what I loved most to win your love (Romans 8:32) and I've waited an eternity for you (Ephesians 1:11). If you believe Me, I will save you (Romans 1:16). I will come to you riding on a white horse (Revelation 19:11) and I will be your champion (Jeremiah 20:11).

I am Jesus, the Lover of your soul.

(Prepared by Cindy at Bethlehem Farms Ministries)

That letter has been a special treasure in my life. I cry every time I read it and am reminded over and over again of God's amazing love for us. What's even more amazing is that God loves us exactly as we are today. We don't have to "become" anything to earn His adoration. If only we could be that easy on ourselves!

A WEDDING TALE

I'll never forget one of the most embarrassing moments in my life. Since I've spent just about half my time walking down the aisle, and the other half recovering from those trips, I just can't resist telling my best "wedding" story!

During the time I was in Los Angeles shooting my TV series *Cover Up,* I had an assistant named Paula. She was a divorced mom of two preteens, levelheaded and independent. One day she burst through the office door with a grin as wide as the Rio Grande. "I'm getting married next weekend, and I want you to be there. I want you to read this poem I wrote during the ceremony. Please, please, please," she squealed as she shoved her "iambic pentameter" at me. My response was one of total surprise. "Next weekend?! Don't you think that's a little rushed? Who is this guy? How long have you known him?! What do your kids think? Are you nuts?" As I heard my own words, I realized how utterly ridiculous those questions were coming from me—the one with a lengthy rap sheet of wedded "unbliss." It occurred to me that I'd spent the majority of my time between marriage and recovery telling my kids, "Don't do as I did; do as I say," and there I was parroting the same sentiment to my grown assistant. Paula assured me that she was making the right decision. She had dated her intended husband for several years, but then he was transferred and had to leave the country. Now he was back for good, her kids adored him, and they were going to make the commitment of marriage. Her enthusiasm was unquenchable, so I decided to zip my lip, attend her wedding, and read the poem for her. I gave her a hug and said no more.

A few days later, Paula called and told me her fiancé was going to send a limousine to take me and another friend of hers to the service. I said the car wasn't necessary, but Paula insisted, and again her excitement overrode my objections. Well, the next Saturday morning we were whisked off in the limo due to arrive a few minutes before the noon wedding. Normally it's a twenty-minute drive from my house to the hotel, but nothing was normal with this particular limo driver. The man must have been in his nineties, was hard of hearing, and barely able to see over the dashboard. He crawled the stretch down the superhighway at a hot thirty-five miles per hour, finally depositing us outside the hotel a half-hour late! I told him we were expected at noon and begged him to "step on it," but nothing I said inspired a faster pace. I was in a total snit when we rushed into the lobby and saw a porter holding up a sign for the wedding. He ushered us into the packed room decorated to the nines and found some seats for us just as Paula was walking down the aisle. I was surprised at how many people were attending, and how formal the service was, because Paula was an extremely laid-back individual. Nonetheless, she was dressed in an exquisite long white gown and veil, with most of the guests elegantly accessorized in cocktail attire. I regarded my simple skirt and blouse and felt totally out of place, in addition to frazzled.

Before I could even catch my breath, the service began. Soon the priest reached the part before their vows where I was to read Paula's poem. I stood, reluctant to break the somber mood, but Paula had been extremely specific in her instructions for me to come forward on the priest's last line, stand in between her and the groom, and read out loud the poem she had written.

I walked boldly down the aisle determined not to disappoint my friend. I made my way to the altar, and with a slight bow, stepped right into the middle of the ceremony. I cleared my throat and began reading the poem in my best Shakespearean voice. Suddenly I felt an arctic freeze cross my back as a disturbed hush fell over the room and all eyes turned on me. I felt excruciatingly awkward, glancing back toward Paula for reassurance. It was then the bride lifted her veil and I realized that it was not Paula! There I was, reading a poem and standing smack-dab in the middle of some stranger's wedding!

I can state with certainty, the color that flushed my face in embarrassment has never been seen on this planet before. My knees buckled, and I literally started stuttering in an attempt to apologize. Then the mother of the bride gasped in a ringing tone across the entire assembly, "I can't believe it—it's Jennifer O'Neill!" She pointed at me like a rare bird in a zoo and then started to clap. At that point, the bride came to life out of her stupor. "Oh, please, Jennifer, keep reading—that was so pretty!" I hesitated, but spurred on by a strong nod of approval from both the priest and the starstruck groom, I read on, trying to give Paula's poem as much theatrical depth as possible. After a couple of false starts I was into it, full tilt!

But not for long. The mood was again broken by a loud *"PSSSST!"* coming from the hallway. And then another *"PSSSST!"* I looked up, irritated that my Academy Award poem performance was being disturbed, and realized it was Paula who was *"psssst*ing" and motioning me away from the ceremony. I waved her off, whispering between gritted teeth that I'd be right with her. I just had to finish this wedding, and then I'd be right there to do hers. But Paula persisted in breaking my flow by walking right into the middle of their wedding! I was horrified! But I was even more horrified when she looked me straight in the eye and said, "Smile, you're on *Celebrity Bloopers and Practical Jokes!* Without skipping a beat I replied, "Smile, you're fired!"

I have to admit it was the best wedding I ever crashed!

FROM FALLEN TO FORGIVEN

God told me in His Word
To let the past go
All my shame, all the pain
All the things that hurt me so

Apologies...
All those people owe me
God told me
To stop holding on

So please forgive me for not forgiving you
Jesus shows me mercy, I'm to show it too
The cross cancels every debt
True love sees us through

From fallen to forgiven
The Holy Spirit leads the way
My comfort, my army
If I become afraid

From fallen to forgiven
I'm feeling brand new
I'm healed by God's love
Delivered by His truth

WORDS BY JENNIFER O'NEILL
MUSIC BY MERVIN LOUQUE & JENNIFER O'NEILL

5

Testing ... One, Two, Three!

Fighting the Good Fight

If you're concerned about being out of control . . .
you're probably not.

—J. O'N

WHEN THE ENEMY TRIES TO MARK ME FOR A FALL, his plan of attack begins by chipping away at an individual weakness; perhaps a little tear in my prayer covering or purpose. If he fails at gaining access to my vulnerable side, he'll try to enter through the back door of my shame and other areas of least resistance that fester in the open sores of unforgiveness. If somehow I still manage to ward him off, he'll pull out the big guns and go straight for the jugular through my relationships and reputation. It took a battlefield full of wounds before I finally learned to follow God's words of protection and empowerment. How? On a daily basis, I put on God's armor and let Him continually heal those areas of vulnerability that the enemy uses against me.

I was getting exhausted emotionally, physically, and spiritually fighting battles I couldn't see or hear to argue against. The war felt deeply internal and deeply disturbing. It was almost as if I were schizophrenic; two conflicting forces vying for my attention, direction, actions, and intentions. I was getting worn out by my own worldly desires, which was just what the enemy had in mind. Almost daily, I would sincerely resolve to change a behavior, attitude, or thought pattern, and the next thing I knew, I was beating myself up for being weak and undisciplined. I didn't know that God does not expect us to do anything without His power, which He explains so clearly in His Word. When I really studied Ephesians 6:13–18 again, I began to see the light and wield a "big stick" by the power of God in Jesus' name:

> Therefore put on the full armor of God, so that when the day of evil comes, you may be able to stand your ground, and after you have done everything, to stand. Stand firm then, with the belt of truth buckled around your waist, with the breastplate of righteousness in place, and with your feet fitted with the readiness that comes from the gospel of peace. In addition to all this, take up the shield of faith, with which you can extinguish all the flaming arrows of the evil one. Take the helmet of salvation and the sword of the Spirit, which is the word of God. And pray in the Spirit on all occasions with all kinds of prayers and requests. With this in mind, be alert and always keep on praying for all the saints.

Putting on the armor of God every day absolutely changed my life. The Scripture powerfully explains what we're up against and how God keeps His word to protect us from the evil one. "Don't leave home without it" is an understatement—putting on your armor is a necessity as you move through God's healing in His will.

Life is all about relationships. It occurred to me that the most important relationships we *do not* have a choice in are with our immediate family. How many bad experiences growing up still rob our todays? How many of our good experiences do we recycle? Where do our friends and business associates fit into our relationship mix, and what is our church family really supposed to mean in our daily lives? What are our relationship choices based on? Need? Fear of being alone? Codependency? Social pressure? How do we heal and grow in the relationships we already have? How do we make solid commitments for the future? Where do we go when we *feel* God has deserted us? How can I be the walking billboard of what doesn't work in relationships, and then be able to turn that negative pattern around to settle on some solid ground?

Do you want to tap into the power of your very own Eveready Spiritual Energizer Bunny? The application of God's instructions in our lives is the only thing that can give us that supernatural power. Being a Christian runs the gamut of emotions from euphoric to humbling, from praising to grumbling, with our sustaining instructions for success in all areas ever present in the Word of God. Still, for me some directions are easier to follow than others. I don't have much trouble with obvious right and wrong, but when situations bump into my bevy of bad habits or old sin nature, it's harder to be obedient. This skid in my resolve runs me off the road at times, even though I know that if I'd apply God's Word to every attitude, thought, or circumstance, the end result would be victory! So why does obedience sometimes feel like I'm throwing myself into a vat of boiling oil? Part of the reason is that escaping our own natural penchant for sin is one of the most difficult challenges we face. It reminds me of a story:

There was a massive flood overtaking the land. On one side of the raging river, all were doomed. Knowing his fate, a scorpion found a frog about to swim to safety across the river and asked the frog for a ride on his back. The frog looked at the lethal being and laughed. "Are you nuts? You're a scorpion. You'll kill me!" But the scorpion argued, "Don't be ridiculous. If I sting you, we'll both die." Accepting his logic, the frog invited the scorpion onto his back and began his way across the river. Halfway to safety, the scorpion fatally stung the frog. As they were both being swallowed by the unforgiving waters, the frog incredulously garbled a last question, "Why did you sting me? Now we're both going to die!" The scorpion simply replied, "It's my nature!"

Let's face it, getting rid of our sin nature is not like changing our clothes; it's like changing our skin. And the only one that breezes through that kind of transformation is a snake!

Letting Go and Letting God

"I can't take it anymore" is a feeling I've had all too often in my life. It didn't matter that I had achieved great career success and commanded relentless drive; eventually my pendulum would swing just a little too far and then crash to a despairing halt. I was doomed. Before I accepted Christ, my feelings were my captain, and my need for love and acceptance charted my course. Although that has changed since coming to faith, at times of trial, the discomfort zone can still be absolutely overwhelming. Not only have I found myself frightened by the onslaught of tests, but the scariest times were when my faith suddenly seemed a distant memory at the hands of distress. But then, God says He will never give us more than we can bear in order to "grow us up" in Him.

I didn't understand or trust the concept of "submission" early on in my faith. The only way I related to giving up my spot at the helm was to let another person have it. I learned the hard

way that was definitely out of the question. Bottom line, submission felt like a walk down death row.

When I'm working my horse, Amazing Grace (nicknamed
"Gracie"), and she takes a deep breath and licks her lips, it
means she's given in to the ride. When I take a deep breath and
lick my lips, it means I'm ready for battle. I was not going to give
in to submission without a fight! The only person I had ever
been able to rely on in the long run was me. That's a rather sad
statement, given the bang-up job I had been doing running my
life. Still, in the scheme of things, "I" was better than no one at
all. At least that's what I had surmised. Enter Jesus Christ. In
many ways the real battle was just about to begin. When a
struggle for control escalates, and life itself hangs in the balance,
it's time to reevaluate who's in charge.

> During the days of Jesus' life on earth, he offered up prayers and
> petitions with loud cries and tears to the one who could save him
> from death, and he was heard because of his reverent submission.
> (Hebrews 5:7)

> Submit yourselves, then, to God. Resist the devil, and he will flee
> from you. (James 4:7)

Submission is such a touchy subject, isn't it? Even the term
seems immediately offensive to our sense of self. In our culture,
we've bought into the popular notion that each of us has an integral right to be happy on demand. It's so much more attractive to
follow our own path. After all, we've been taught to mythologize
ourselves and rely on ourselves for everything, including our
"spiritual growth." Just aspire to a higher conscious level, and in
the end we'll evolve into "oneness" with the ultimate conscious

level: God. Therefore, we become God! Pretty cool, huh? The only problem is, it's not the truth. We are not God; we are His children. He's the boss, thank God! I have finally given up running for the office of being in charge of the world. I have finally stopped negotiating with God. I spent most of my life wanting to do things my way while bringing new meaning to the word *impatient*. That attitude only brought me unhappiness and several times almost cost me my life. God loves us enough to discipline us even if we don't like it, and He'll leave us out there as long as we insist on having it our own way. Yet, if we rest in Him, submit, and let Him drive, He will bring all things around to our good.

SAV-BABY

I have a dear new friend, Donna DeSoto, who found me through my Web site. She has an extraordinary story. After a near-death experience, God told Donna that she could return to her life if she would follow the mission He had set for her—to save His babies. Through the power of the Lord for the last ten years, this terrific lady has been doing just that with her national campaign to save abandoned infants and restore families. I have been privileged to be a part of her mission by helping make her voice heard on a broader basis. To that end, I'm producing her story as a TV Movie of the Week, *SAV-BABY*. While working on this venture, Donna and I have become very close. Together we look to God for His power and timetable for the project. (By the way, God's the best agent I've ever had!) Donna and I both sport freight-train personalities, and as it happens, both our husbands have much more laid-back meters. It's probably not a coincidence that our collective marriages are true tests of the notion that opposites attract. Recently, the news of my finding the right company, director, and approach for the SAV-BABY project ignited Donna and me to squeals of joy and mountains of praise for God's handiwork. But something was robbing that joy, and when I shared my feelings with Donna, I learned she was experiencing the same power drainage. Both our husbands, in their own ways, seemed distant, unsupportive, and at times even angry. Beyond a wet blanket, it felt like a drowning to both of us. I went into my prayer warrior mode. God's answer was one of His basic truths, "Leave your husband and any work necessary in him to Me and focus on your own areas of needed repair." God had whispered this into my spirit. Happily, this time I heard Him loud and clear.

I called Donna and shared how God had chastened me, and at once we both repented in a duet of confession. Now, the truth be known, this rebuke from our Lord was really tough for both of us. I said, "Donna, we have to step back, let our husbands take a breath, not respond to any negativity from them, and wait on God to do a work in them. Our only lament should be, 'God change *me* . . . What do I have to realign?' Meanwhile, we have to present ourselves to our husbands as godly wives, gentle in spirit and respectful. God promises He'll take care of the rest." It was beyond difficult for two loudmouths like Donna and me to calm down and stop pointing fingers at our husbands' lack of enthusiasm, but we did, and with the power of the Holy Spirit, it worked. There was a release for all of us in respect to the refining God wanted to do in each of our lives as well as in our lives as couples. (Stereo works in progress!) The enemy is foiled on a day-to-day basis by our obedience.

Donna's and my effectiveness for the project was not diminished, but was put in right relationship with how God intended us to proceed. When we recognize that anger, disappointments, insecurities, or feelings of abandonment are not of God, and we let Him be Lord of our lives, our joy is safe no matter what or who lets us down . . . even if it's our husbands! Of course, the same holds true in reverse, when we let them down, which invariably we will in some way or other. We're all just imperfect people after all.

I find that so many of us at some point in our marriages turn and look at our spouses and think, *Who the heck are you, and how did you get into my life?* First off, our husbands are who they've always been minus the smooth "date" wrapping we all seem to shed after the I do's are professed. If I'm honest when looking back on my failed marriages, there existed a strong indication of the worst nightmares in store for me at the hands of some of those men, but I chose to ignore the warning signs. "Oh, he'll get over that," or "I'll change that later on," was my mantra. (By the way, the same applied to what they would experience with me!) What about our "after-the-honeymoon's-over" wail, "How did you get into my life?"? We invited them in! Not only that, we made them dinner and dessert, to boot. Once we finally own our part of the "rose-colored courtship" that has the potential of turning on us like a crazed pit bull, let's put the muzzle on ourselves and take care of what *we* need to do to forgive and heal into wholeness. (Asking for forgiveness should also be at the top of our list.)

A RIGHT RELATIONSHIP

As a kid in school, I trusted report cards because those grades would let me know in black and white where I stood in the scheme of things and where I needed to improve. Fortunately, now my desire to please God is not born of the same old frenetic need to earn love. In accepting His unconditional love, I have also accepted His promises, not the least of which is to be empowered to fulfill *His* will in my life. So the task has become: How can I actually increase my goals, set timetables to them, stay engaged in growth, track my progress, and clearly define God's will?

Guess what? The Word says that I can do none of the above things without the Holy Spirit's guidance to healing, which is impossible without first dealing with my unforgiveness! I found out that God offers absolutely no shortcuts to this truth. I was just going to have to face the facts and face God's command.

Again, God says in the Lord's Prayer that I must forgive so I will be forgiven (Matthew 6:14–15)—only then will I completely heal and be released from the bondage of my past. God says that I must ask the Holy Spirit in prayer to show me my true and hidden places of unforgiveness so I can discern the truth from the enemy's lies. God says I must recognize my areas of needed healing according to His Word and accept responsibility for everything I think, say, and do. It is for me to decide and choose to be released from my unforgiveness that holds me to my painful past and negative patterns. If I don't, God says I won't experience an entire or true healing, spiritual growth, or a release of His full will in my life. I must trust God as my protector and partner in my forgiving and healing process, and only the power of the Holy Spirit will enable me, comfort me, and supply all my needs as I proceed. I can do none of this on my own! Jesus has paid the price for every one of my sins— past, present, and future. He loves me unconditionally wherever I am—now—and has declared my personal worthiness by His sacrifice for me. If I hold on to unforgiveness of others or myself, I do not have a lack of real faith and trust in God and His promises. Grace is not a commodity; rather, grace is the

Lord God Himself. Quickness in obedience, compassion, and mercy are the keys to forgiving others through the leadership and power of the Holy Spirit. I must not withhold forgiveness of anyone—but that does not mean that I have to "do business" with that person again! Nor does that person have to agree or participate in my forgiveness of him or her. God says that this truth also includes the deceased who have left our lives. I must have true faith, which is not a belief in faith, but rather faith in God. I must be in right relationship with the author of love—God.

GOD'S WILL AND MY WAY!

The will of God will never take us where our faith won't sustain us. The will of God depends on faith when things look impossible and feel out of control. God loves to do His work in our lives at the very last moment just to be sure we recognize that in Him, we can do all things, but without Him we are not only eternally lost, we are ultimately powerless. Yes, those mighty uncomfortable trials and tests do bring us into His will. So, I've won the war of salvation, but how do I stop losing daily battles?

> Therefore, since we have been justified through faith, we have peace with God through our Lord Jesus Christ, through whom we have gained access by faith into this grace in which we now stand. And we rejoice in the hope of the glory of God. Not only so, but we also rejoice in our sufferings, because we know that suffering produces perseverance; perseverance, character; and character, hope. And hope does not disappoint us, because God has poured out his love into our hearts by the Holy Spirit, whom he has given us. (Romans 5:1–5)

The word *sufferings* refers to all kinds of trials that may press in on us. This includes such things as the pressures of financial or physical need, trying circumstances, sorrow, sickness, persecution, mistreatment, or loneliness. In the middle of these troubles God's grace enables us to seek His face more diligently and produces in us a persevering spirit and character that overcome the trials of life. Change does come from pain, but still, we all know "old habits die hard." Could I finally grow up without getting bashed over the head or hospitalized with a broken heart? It was going to be my choice. In the end, the only one who was going to change was me. I was the work in progress, not God.

With all of the healing that is waiting to be unleashed upon our request, the stretch marks of "tests and trials" suddenly pale next to the wholeness and victory of His deliverance that is worth every painful step of the way! It's a whole new world when we arrive at the point of suffering trials and instead of running away, we enthusiastically look toward what we are to learn. When I work with women (as well as girls), most of the issues that need to be addressed surface in the area of relationships; past, present, potential, and so often, painfully poisonous. Maybe that's why God has called me as a messenger of this "spiritual journey into wholeness and healing." Since relationships were always my downfall, I know well their pitfalls and pains.

Sometimes after my speaking engagements, groups of ladies stay on to talk out their personal issues. Although cast with different names and stories, their hurts are so often pointed squarely at their husbands' shortcomings and behavior. Clearly, this is because a spouse represents such a huge part of a woman's life. Although I ache for these women who feel unheard, unappreciated, ignored, cheated, or abused (physically or verbally), I know God's directions are to keep bringing them back to His clear instruction: Face *your* unforgiveness through the power of the Holy Spirit, give *all* your painful relationships back to Him, and God will do the necessary work in them. Then the job at hand is what is in *your* control . . . YOU and your issues!

Okay, it's time to remind you again that you're not alone . . . *You're not alone!* By the way, if your heart is pounding nervously, the good news is that you're still alive. The bad news is that you're probably still holding on to the places where you hide. The first thing we must reroute is our methods of escape. You're going to be amazed at how ingenious we can be at hide-and-seek!

But before we begin, here's a bit of levity, a vignette of how a game of hide-and-seek can teach us to have a better sense of humor about ourselves! When Merve and I married, we did it God's way, abstaining from sex prior to marriage. I was able to stand before God and my husband fresh and new. That's something for a (then) forty-eight-year-old with three grandchildren, many failed marriages, and thirty-eight years of life without knowing Christ. God is so gracious!

Merve and I entertained the idea of having our own child (quickly, as my clock was about ticked out), but it was only a fleeting thought, especially when I recalled the story about a woman who gave birth to her first child at fifty years old. She was so excited about her miracle, and she asked all her friends over to see the little bundle of joy. When everyone gathered with great anticipation in her living room, the woman suddenly looked panicked! She had forgotten where she put her baby! (Just another daily adventure on the not-so-merry-menopause-go-round!) Luckily, God never forgets where He puts us!

FOREVERMORE

You have the way
That makes me come alive
You have the words
That move me deep inside
And I have this love of mine . . .
Only for you

I'm still a child of the heart
Still a child of the heart

That nevermore—will I feel afraid
And nevermore—will I turn away
And in Your arms (I'm believing—You'll never leave me)
I can rest (and now it feels like we can be)
Forevermore

I have this heart
That follows You everywhere
I have this faith
That holds me when I get scared
And I have this love of mine
Only for You

I'm still a child of the heart
Still a child of the heart

That nevermore—will I feel afraid
And nevermore—will I turn away
And in Your arms (I'm believing—You'll never leave me)
I can rest (and now it feels like we can be)
Forevermore

WORDS AND MUSIC BY JENNIFER O'NEILL.
HANDSHAKE PRODUCTIONS.
USED BY PERMISSION.

6

Untying God's Ribbon

Opening the Gift of His Power

What part of integrity can we lose for gain
and still stay intact? None!
—J. O'N

NOT TOO LONG AFTER I HAD GONE THROUGH THE
immense drama and trauma in my own life of losing a child
through abortion, I found myself back in the "real world" and
visiting Japan as a guest of a celebrity tennis tournament. On
our day off, I went sightseeing to the outskirts of Tokyo. The
largest Buddhist temple in the countryside sat nestled in a valley
surrounded by rolling hills as far as the eye could see. There in
front of me was an amazing sight. Thousands and thousands of
pinwheels were stuck in the ground (remember the twirling plas-
tic miniature windmills on a stick that we put in our hats or on
our bikes as kids?). Imagine these countless pinwheels neatly
lined up row after row after row, flowing past the horizon. Next
to each pinwheel were hand-knitted baby booties and *empty* picture frames, along with mementos and keepsakes of every kind.
I found out that these were all offerings to the miniature graves
of aborted Japanese babies!

My heart broke at the loss. After the initial shock of what I was looking at eased, something occurred to me. Because most Japanese people believe in reincarnation, they at least recognize and grieve their aborted babies as lost lives. They acknowledge the child's soul, unlike most of the world, where the atrocity of abortion is all too often sloughed off as easily as a toothache after going to the dentist. But in truth, I was to learn that abortion leaves your soul ripped apart, ravaged by guilt and shame that deeply haunt your heart. I was also to learn that in Christ, forgiveness and healing exist for even this act of devastation, as long as the experience is not shoved away in some unbelieving, forgotten place of denial and pain. I see so many women devastated by the abortions they've regretfully had—but there is hope and help for them. I can personally attest to that. Jack Hayford, in his powerful book *I'll Hold You in Heaven*, speaks lovingly of the little ones lost, saying in fact that every child who is aborted, miscarried, stillborn, or dies an early death exists. These children are with God as eternal souls and are capable of spiritual, sensitive communication. He goes on to remind us that "each unborn being has viable spiritual sensitivity. Although intellect and speech as we know it may not have begun, sensitivity, spiritual potential and distinctly human capacities are present. God places inestimable value on these, and, at death, the infant passes into the presence of God . . ."

There is such comfort in these words. When we put our trust in God, even our biggest mistakes, tragedies, and unimaginable sins can truly become "trials turned to gold" through the power of the Holy Spirit.

TOTAL WELL-BEING

We've talked about relationships, their complexities, their influence, their importance. The health of our relationships with one another is as integral to our well-being as our physical, emotional, and spiritual health. That's why "wholeness" is so necessary. If we've finally embraced our happiness and fulfillment in life, but are suddenly stricken with a fatal disease, it will be hard to enjoy the fruits of our labor. Our total well-being is the goal.

Dr. O. S. Hawkins describes three primary relationships in our lives as: Outward (with one another), Inward (with ourselves), and Upward (with God). All three are vital to our continuing personal growth. For us to be living outside of a right relationship with God is like committing suicide when we're already dead—double jeopardy!

How do we truly feel about our Father in heaven, and how do we forgive the unforgivable and unforgotten? Here are some questions to consider and honestly answer for yourself:

1. At my core, do I really believe God is good, or am I disappointed in Him?

2. Do I really believe God can heal my biggest nightmares and weakest points?

3. Do I really believe that God truly has my best interests at heart?

4. Do I really trust that He will empower and protect me?

5. Do I underestimate what God wants to do through me?

I've already talked about my own coming to a crossroads with God six years ago. It was a period of time when I didn't trust Him. I thought God had let me down, lied to me, abandoned me, and didn't hear my cries of anguish. I felt invisible and unloved, similar to when I was a child, but this was even worse. If God wasn't what He promised to be, where could I turn? I have never felt such loneliness as during that period of disconnect with my Creator. Thank goodness it was a short estrangement! I was literally suffocating without my faith. Once I stopped pointing my finger at my Father in heaven, I realized that I had been trying to run my life my way, in His name. God wasn't about to let me pull that junk with Him. He showed me a sliver of His power just to cement our relationship and tide me over, as my big-time "molding-shaping" season still lay ahead. God knew I was going to need a dose of spiritual adrenaline to get me through my next chapter or two.

Dr. James Dobson, in his book *The Betrayal Barrier,* talks about the phenomenon of shattered faith. It's an agony he says few other circumstances in living can equal—and in fact, it happens in 100 percent of believers. We might lose a job, or a child— or we just begin realizing that life is unraveling and nothing makes sense anymore. We question God's love and care and in return question our love for Him. Dobson calls it a tragic misunderstanding. His book states that more than 90 percent of us fail to break through this betrayal barrier after feeling abandoned by God. We must come to terms with our own "betrayal barriers" so that our faith will not be hindered.

UP IN SMOKE

Did I really believe God could heal me? No . . . not until He graciously called my bluff and answered one of my prayers. I have to admit, I only halfheartedly prayed, "God, please lift this demon of smoking off me. I have tried by my might and discipline, but I keep failing over and over again. Help me, Lord."

I had smoked cigarettes since I was sixteen years old. When I started, no one said smoking could be harmful. There were no Surgeon General Warnings on the cigarette packs and no campaigns on the dangers of this addictive habit. Smoking was advertised as "cool" on TV and in magazines, with everyone who was anyone from movie stars to major athletes puffing away. Cigarettes were part of my being, an ever-present physical appendage to my personality. It was impossible to consider ending a meal without a puff or twenty, let alone having a conversation on the phone, being creative, or going through a trauma without that ever-soothing ring of smoke, a lethal halo over my head. I loved cigarettes, and they had always been good to me, both by controlling my weight and making me feel hip. I didn't suffer the usual downsides of smoking—as a competitive athlete, I showed and trained my horses without even a hint of breathless malfunction.

So why did my seemingly cool habit need to go up in smoke? Even once I had accepted Christ in my life, I continued smoking, but when I started to make Jesus Lord of my life, I noticed that Mr. Cigarette occupied a lot more of my attention than he should! It was getting harder and harder to deny the downsides of smoking: cancer, emphysema, heart disease, death—just for starters. Then one day I heard a voice as clearly as if it were right next to me, *"Jennifer, you're pressing your luck. This little habit of yours is really going to stop you dead in your tracks before you've run your race. Quit it, now!"* I recognized that God was seriously talking to me, and He got my attention. The only problem was, I could not seem to quit! All my resolve, my methods of handling withdrawal, my "covering up" when I would mess up, became very time-consuming and belied my desire to put God first in my life.

Fast-forward to my healing. Boom! One day I prayed, yet again, a pathetic little prayer of half belief to God. He answered me, despite myself. Every other time I had tried to quit smoking,

I ended up feeling sorry for myself. Then, through the Holy Spirit's power, I suddenly realized it wasn't about feeling sorry for myself, it was about loving myself. I wanted freedom from this wall between me and God's will for my life. It became a matter of respecting my potential in God's eyes. Here's the most amazing, miraculous part: God simply obliterated my cigarette demon. Gone . . . up in smoke . . . never to rear its ugly head again!

God just loves to hear our praise, thanksgiving, and applause for His power in our lives! Go, God, go! So, with a wave of His mighty hand, I was an instantaneous smoke-free believer in miracles!

No Doubt About It!

Soon I was checking "believing God can heal" off my doubt list, but what about the rest? Did I really think God had my best interests at heart? That stumbling block wasn't an easy one to step over either. I had to admit "no" was my answer to that question, as well. How could God have my best interests at heart when He wasn't making my life happen the way I had scripted it? My leading men continued to turn into villains; my dreams, schemes, and finances were methodically fading away; and if I had three deals on the table, four would fall apart. *What's up, God? I don't call allowing one disaster after another having my best interests at heart!* Nothing seemed to be going my way! Wasn't I supposed to be fulfilled and bountiful in His grace? This felt worse than PMS and menopause all wrapped up together!

So, how did I finally get over myself—a self that reminded me of the hysterical babies we always run into at the grocery store? I stopped crying, whining, and moaning, changed my dirty diaper of despair, and put on a new attitude. As soon as I quieted down, I realized that God had already put me in a better place than I had ever dreamed of . . . I had His unconditional love, protection, care, and a plan for me that was the "part of a lifetime"!

That's two down on the Doubt Poll and two biggies to go. Had I really trusted that God would empower and protect me? Suffering what seemed to be an endless time of trials and misfortune, I continued to yearn for the relief of God's covering. I felt bedraggled and weak, unprotected and meek. None of the cards in my hands were winners or even a good bluff. I was experiencing another dry season that seemed void of all hope or relief.

RIGHT WHERE GOD WANTED ME TO BE

On the heels of my divorce from Richard, I was thrown into my own real-life "southern trial," which only exaggerated all my helpless feelings. With thirteen court postponements and the press's slander of my reputation severing my ability to work, I fell deeper into despair. At the last moment, like the Lone Ranger riding into the courtroom and sweeping me away from danger, God saved the day. He held me from harm's way, answered my prayers with a bellowing "not guilty," and I was no longer "theirs" for the picking. No doubt, God was at work in His supernatural grace and protection of me. I felt so loved and relieved, despite my total state of disarray. Still, the question remained: Did I believe God would really empower me now that He had shown me His protection?

All my "toys" had been taken away and every method of my "independence" had been dislodged and rendered useless. Every one of my hiding places was exposed and disinfected, every expression of personal power I had flexed on a regular basis now atrophied from loss of use. Stripped naked, I finally turned it all over to God and sincerely asked Him to show me His will in my life. This was not an easy rollover on my part, as I was feeling little to no confidence or peace of mind at the time. Rather, I was agitated, intermittently angry, scared to death, in withdrawal of my former life, and totally helpless.

The truth is, I was right where God wanted me to be so He could do His next work in me. That is when He began to empower me for His purpose.

From the world's view I was down, but from God's view, I was not out. In fact, I was just beginning. God allowed me to write *Surviving Myself* with an honesty that He used to cleanse me and reach others. It was a scary, cathartic time, but He gave me a daily dose of fortitude in Him, and then sent me out of the nest to use my testimony for His glory. Do I believe God will empower me? If I am in His will, I am in His power! I believe that none of us who are in God's will die before His entire plan for our lives is realized—not by disease, world influences, spiritual warfare, or unequally yoked relationships. What a relief!

Do I underestimate what God wants to do through me? Up until recently I would have to admit, yes, I did. It was beyond my imagination what God had in mind for me. My potential in His will is limitless because He is limitless, and that was a new concept for me. It isn't about how good I am, but rather, *How great He is!* As long as I stay in daily prayer for covering, expansion, empowerment, discernment, obedience, and protection from the enemy, I will continue to grow in Him, through the power of the Holy Spirit and the blood of Jesus.

Now What?

When God closes a door in our lives, and hasn't yet opened a new one (by *our* definition), it can be extremely uncomfortable. Waiting on God was a lesson I learned very well about two years ago. My autobiography was written and released, and I had just finished a national talk show publicity campaign. After I took a breath, there I sat, wondering, *What's next?* My life story was optioned in Hollywood to make a TV Movie of the Week, but at the end of the day, I withdrew the project because the network insisted on its right to fictionalize portions of my life, even those included in the book. If there was ever a life that didn't need to have any spice, danger, or compelling issues added, it was mine! I certainly wouldn't recommend to my parents or children that they sign away their rights to some stranger's imagination, especially since that "stranger from a strange town" might be more intent on high ratings than integrity of the story. There was also the concern that the TV script would not reflect my story's real message and balance, a story of survival through faith, not "tabloid and headlines." I was advised that the network's focus would likely be on the "sensational" and "dramatic" aspects of *Surviving Myself*, rather than on my ultimate victory in Christ.

What made passing on this deal particularly tough was the loss of substantial income that would have come from it. Nonetheless, I turned it down, trusting that God would open some other door of opportunity for me to support my family. I waited . . . ever the impatient one . . . I waited. Then, out of the blue, I received a booking to tell my testimony at an enormous gathering sponsored by the Salvation Army. I was ecstatic! I called my husband, and with gibbering excitement, told him the grand news. "See, Merve," I gushed. "God answered my prayers!" What an important booking . . . what an honor. I was ready . . . a little scared, *no, a lot scared*, but ready. Everything would be okay; I had a couple of months to study. My husband was thrilled for me, and I dived into courses on public speaking to prepare for my August engagement.

That's when the contract arrived in the mail. It was the beginning of June 1998, and I had cleared my calendar for August 15. When I read the official confirmation, it was for August 15, 1999—more than one year away! Well, I wailed, I moaned, I cried out to God. "No, I'm ready *now!* Who knows if I'll even be alive in 1999? I have to have the income now!" I was off on one of my old bratty tirades, giving God a piece of my mind and letting Him know that He was taking too long to do everything in my life!

As you might imagine, August 15, 1999, came before I knew it, and as I stood on the Salvation Army's amphitheater stage giving my testimony, I realized that I was barely ready then, certainly not a year before, as I had protested. I also realized that God knows how impatient I am. In His loving knowledge of me, He let me have a peek into the future by showing me that faraway booking so I'd settle down and prepare for my mission. I like my new tune: "God is never late. (*Oh no, don't clock Him.*) God is good. (*Oh yes, as I've never known.*) God's got my number. (*Oh boy, and He's called me on it.*) And God loves me anyway. (*Oh yes, He loves me anyway!*)"

I've been speaking my testimony of the transforming love of God all over the country for the last couple of years. If you're wondering, yes, once I let Him, God has provided for all my needs—spiritually, financially, and directorially. I am totally flabbergasted at how I ever spent one day on this earth without His grace and love. Allowing God to work in our lives is our choice, and He will do so in direct correlation to our personal relationship with Him and our request and trust in Him.

God sent His Son to die for us, His Holy Spirit to convict and empower us, and His unconditional love to forgive and heal everything that affects us.

God's party isn't one you'll want to miss. It is an RSVP affair of the heart, so please respond quickly so a place in heaven will be saved in your name!

SHE PRAYS

She cut her hair, changed perfume
Rearranged her room again
Counting sheep, she's losing sleep
Morning comes too soon for her

She prays to God
Lord, I love him so
Bring my husband home
Bring my husband home

Every night, she waits for him
In the name of love
She lets him in
He says he cares, but he's not really there
And the lying never ends

She prays to God
Lord, I love him so
Bring my husband home
Bring my husband home

Years have past
Still her tears never dried
She waits alone
Knowing God will hear her cry

Please forgive me, is now on his lips
Is now on his lips
As he kneels to kiss her hand once more
The fool that let her go
Now prays she understands

She prays to God
Lord, I love him so
Bring my husband home
Bring my husband home

WORDS AND MUSIC BY JENNIFER O'NEILL.
HANDSHAKE PRODUCTIONS.
USED BY PERMISSION.

7

Excuses, Escapes, and Epitaphs

A Little Confession Is Good for the Soul

"Blockbuster" is not a movie but a mind-set.
We just may have to change the way we think to grow.

—J. O'N

THEY CALL IT THE "CHRISTIAN WALK." I CALL IT
the intermittent crawl, sprint, and long-distance marathon of
pratfalls and possibilities. Some turns of the course can be
downright exhausting! What happened to the spirited "giddyup
in our getalong"? Where is all that passion we had when we first
met Christ? Have you observed a newborn Christian recently?
That explosive smile and boundless joy sometimes make me
want to spit, especially when my next leap of faith presents itself
before I've caught my breath from the last one. Let's face it, the
"molding-shaping" periods hurt like crazy and never seem to
end. But I finally figured out that this "God thing" (as my unbelieving friends refer to the change in me) was not a passing
fancy, but rather an invitation to attend the burial of the old
fleshly me, and to move up to the coming-out party of Jennifer,
daughter of God. Talk about stubbed toes and glass slippers!

Driveways in Nashville are covered with a material called
"Crush and Run." I first thought "Crush and Run" was a highway

accident, but now I know it is a basecoat laid before permanent driveways are poured. This "Crush and Run" is a purposeful first layer that prepares the area of travel and, over time, becomes firm, unswayable, and hard as concrete, creating a road that can accommodate any size load. It is the same with our walk with God—one step at a time in creating an unswayable foundation. I want my walk with God to follow a path of least resistance, to be able to carry any load, and provide solid footing with no washouts allowed. If you see me walking around wearing a construction helmet, you'll know why.

It may sound as though I'm getting a handle on my spiritual walk, but please, let me assure you that I continue to have my share of times when I'm not only stuck in gear, but in rush-hour traffic with the shift broken off in my hand! What's particularly threatening during a "stall" is that if we try to step out of our dilemma, we fear getting crushed by oncoming traffic. That's when we start thinking of excuses to deal with our meltdown. "Experts" in this field of denial can actually sell themselves on the notion that they are not in danger, or worse, that they are incapable of making a change for the better and are doomed to wither away. These procrastinators are wrapped like a nut roll in layers of excuses and escapes that only lead to emotional death. If you fall under the heading of "perfectionist," you are doomed to failure because in your estimation, nothing will ever be perfect, so why even bother? Then there are those who are feeling the discomfort of their pain, so instead of change they decide to take a little numbing action; a pill, a drink, a drug, a shopping spree, an affair, followed by a bout of depression and general devastation. The lengths to which we go to hide and avoid are Olympic in proportion and weave a trail of destruction through our lives and the lives of those around us.

SHOW AND TELL

I used to love show and tell when I was a kid in school. It's not quite as much fun when you're grown up! When I realized that the "confess" part of God's process of forgiveness to healing was a mandatory step along the way to my wholeness in Him, I suddenly looked like "yard art"—I was paralyzed with shame and fear. Even just scanning my areas of accountability was torture, let alone calling my failures out by name!

> Therefore confess your sins to each other and pray for each other so that you may be healed. The prayer of a righteous man is powerful and effective. (James 5:16)

Fear paralyzes and robs us of our ability to move forward. I've learned that when I'm feeling fear regarding any issue in my life, it is not from God. I can gain victory as I remember the encouragement in His Word.

> For God hath not given us the spirit of fear; but of power, and of love, and of a sound mind. (2 Timothy 1:7 KJV)

God knows all our deepest, darkest secrets, no matter how fancy our footwork has been in trying to hide them. Until we fess up to all of it, our unforgiveness will spread like a cancer. We have to microscopically x-ray our hearts, minds, and souls, and surgically remove every speck of "dirt" through the power of the Holy Spirit so an infection won't spread over our futures or to our loved ones. The origin of our pain authors our excuses and designs our hiding places. Challenge the enemy's strongholds that grip your life by first recognizing the areas they reside in, both in your past and your present, so that they won't own your future.

EXCUSES, EXCUSES

Do any of the enemy's excuses sound familiar to you? "I regret I will be unable to attend my healing because . . . I'm out of town" "Who's on the guest list?" "I prefer my own parties," "I don't have the proper attire," "I can't afford a gift," "I'm not sure what fork to use," "I don't have a date," "I'm feeling ugly today," "I'm having a bad hair day," "Oops, raging hormones," "I have the flu (and so do my kids and my dog)," . . . or, "I'm just too busy being busy." When the rubber meets the road, we don't want to get left in the dust or run out of gas. With all our sidestepping suppression and avoidance of the truth, it's not surprising that we feel drained when we get up, and sad when we lie down.

Let's tackle once and for all one of the biggest excuses known to man (and woman): "I can't help it; it's their fault. They did it to me!" As I mentioned earlier, the most important relationships we don't have a choice in are those with our family. We do not have to inherit, be crippled by, accept, or pass on generational sin! No more band-aids, blind spots, or baggage! This is my prayer:

Dear Lord,

I know that when I go to a medical doctor's office, they ask for my family history so they can best care for me. I know that if a disease or any type of ailment has afflicted my family's past generations, then I must take special care to guard myself and my family from inherited genetic weaknesses that could adversely affect our health and well-being. But what about spiritually?

Father God, You are the all-powerful Creator of yesterday, today, and tomorrow, and You say in Your Word that, through the power of the Holy Spirit, I can break the bondage of passed-along generational sin. Thank You, God, for sending Your Son to die for all our sins, and according to Your Word, that includes all generational sin that the enemy would have me, my family, or loved ones inherit.

I come before You, Father God, through the power and sword of the Holy Spirit, and ask You to cut us free from all generational, inherited sins of every nature. According to Your power, promise, and Word, I sever from the dawn of creation any and all spirits, human traits or tendencies, actions, thoughts, connections, relationships, or influences that are not of You! I put the cross covered with the blood of Jesus between us and our parents and grandparents back to the beginning of time and render powerless any relationship that is not of You. By the authority of God's Word, I bind every evil spirit NOW! Anger, sorrow, rage, jealousy, violence, sexual perversion, impurity and promiscuity, cruelty, selfishness, low self-esteem, fear, rejection, doubt, unbelief, hopelessness, criticism, depression, denial, weakness, guilt, gossip, aggression, passivity, addictions, suicidal thoughts or actions, physical, mental, or spiritual disorders are hereby bound and thrown into the fiery pit of hell, in Jesus Christ's name! Thank You, Father God, for this release, protection, and freedom through the power of the Holy Spirit and the blood, resurrection, and name of our Lord and Savior, Jesus Christ. I will claim this victory daily as I put on the armor of God. Amen!

I firmly believe that generational sin and bondage can be broken through prayer because God says it can. I stand in agreement with you on the promises of our Lord for protection in this area, for guidance and the softening of our hearts and those of our children and loved ones. No more negative hand-me-downs for the children of God!

OPENING OUR HEARTS AND
LIVES TO GOD'S WILL

A fairly new relationship in my life has shown me the myriad and mysterious ways God works to bring us and others into His truth.

I was being courted to do business with a gentleman of enormous power and influence. He possessed a rare balance of corporate clout and creative sensibilities, and I was excited at the prospect of working with him. I try to witness to everyone from cabdrivers to studio heads, and this man was no exception. He was of Jewish background and tradition, yet seemed marginally open to discussing Jesus Christ as Savior.

One day he called me from New York and said, "Can I ask you something?" His voice had an unusual ring to it.

"Sure," I answered.

He continued, "I had an experience in Los Angeles that I'm curious about. I went with a bunch of people to a . . . gathering of . . . a . . . ."

"A prayer meeting?" I guessed.

"Yes," he said, "at someone's house. And when I walked into the room there was a guy . . . a man . . . what do they call . . . ?"

"A pastor," I offered.

He hesitated for an instant. "Yes, a pastor. We had arrived late and the pastor had already finished speaking, but the instant he noticed me at the door, he waved for me to come over to him."

I laughed because this was not a man you "wave over." "What did you do?"

"Well," he said, "I did go over to him. We were introduced and the pastor asked straight out if there was something he could pray with me about because I seemed to need prayer."

I held the phone tighter to my ear, not wanting to miss a word. He continued with some urgency.

"I told the pastor that my father had just died, and that's when it happened."

"What happened?!" I was excited.

"Well, the pastor put his hand on my shoulder . . . and the next thing I knew, I was flat out on the floor! What was that?"

I exhaled. "It sounds like you were slain in the Spirit. Personally, I've never been slain in the Spirit. That's so exciting!" Now he was really confused.

"Why? What is 'slain in the Spirit'?"

I explained. "I'm told it's when people become so physically overwhelmed with the presence of the Holy Spirit on them that, in essence, they pass out. The reason this is so interesting to me is that I've seen people slain in the Spirit, but I was never really sure if they just got carried away, or if they were really 'knocked out' by the Holy Spirit. You're a nonbeliever . . . a pastor prays over you and the next thing, you've fallen flat-out cold on the floor. What an invitation to the Lord's power! God waited thirty-eight years for me to accept Christ, but God knocks you flat out to get your attention! That's a pretty powerful tap on the shoulder, don't you think?"

There was a pause in the conversation and I could almost envision this man's thoughts racing through his head.

"When did this happen to you?" I was sure he was ready to receive Christ.

"Two years ago," he mumbled.

"Two years ago?!" I was stunned. All of a sudden I could feel him withdraw; his voice hardened with his next defensive words.

"Look, Jennifer, I know God has His hand on my shoulder. I feel it! I know He's calling me, but I'm not ready to answer. I like my life the way it is. I'm not ready to give up my lifestyle . . . my fun."

My heart sank. What an excuse to ignore God's pursuit. I tried to explain that the only thing God wants from us is our sin. Life doesn't become stifled, boring, and dull when Christ lives in us; rather it abounds with grace, forgiveness, healing, love, and eternal life! Unfortunately, this man was not ready to give up his passing fancies—and the conversation was over. By the way, so were our business opportunities. I never heard from him again. I often think of him and continue to pray for his salvation.

For every action there is a consequence, and for every "excuse" there is a failure to act, which bears a new set of consequences!

If anyone would come after me, he must deny himself and take up his cross daily and follow me. For whoever wants to save his life will lose it, but whoever loses his life for me will save it. (Luke 9:23–24)

"If I knew where I was going, I'd know which way to turn," is one of my most thoughtful lyrical hooks. Not long after enjoying the crafty twist on words, I had to digest them as they presently applied to me. If I *know* where I am going "in faith," I'll *know* which way to turn "in Christ." I'll put away last season's excuses, no matter how comfortable they feel. In the long run, excuses only seem to put off the inevitable and keep us bound to our past.

For years, I treaded murky waters with unseen peril swimming beneath, ready to devour me! I wanted to be cleansed of my fears and the enemy's evil strongholds so I could stop laying myself out as a spiritual sacrifice. I am responsible . . . I'm busted . . . I call myself on all the games I've played and dealt. I have no more excuses. Christ already died for every single sin and need of mine. In Him, this baby doesn't get thrown out with the bathwater; only my excuses and denials do. I'm going to put a checklist next to my prayer list and honestly see how I need to grow in Christ. I'm moving on up the road to victory by the healing power of the Holy Spirit!

Unlike my friend in the "slain in the spirit" story, we have Christ in us and the power of the Holy Spirit to step us through forgiveness to healing. So let's dump all our excuses, get solid in our faith, engage God's Word, claim His will in our lives, and insist on a clean spiritual bill of health!

> His divine power has given us everything we need for life and godliness through our knowledge of him who called us by his own glory and goodness. Through these he has given us his very great and precious promises, so that through them you may participate in the divine nature and escape the corruption in the world caused by evil desires. For this very reason, make every effort to add to your faith *goodness;* and to goodness, *knowledge;* and to knowledge, *self-control;* and to self-control, *perseverance;* and to perseverance, *godliness;* and to godliness, *brotherly kindness;* and to brotherly kindness, *love.* For if you possess these qualities in increasing measure, they will keep you from being ineffective and unproductive in your knowledge of our Lord Jesus Christ. But if anyone does not have them, he is nearsighted and blind, and has forgotten that he has been cleansed from his past sins. (2 Peter 1:3–9, emphasis added)

WWW.GOD.CALM

It takes two to keep company
It takes two to tango
It takes two to sing in harmony
But it takes one to let go

Have you ever felt together alone
With God you're safe
You're always at home
www.God.calm means
You're never alone

It takes lessons to learn
It takes time to grow
It takes hearts to yearn
It takes seeds to sow

Have you ever felt together alone
With God you're safe
You're always at home
www.God.calm means
You're never alone

Peace comes when we let go
Trust comes when we believe
True love is always free
Faith is something we can't see

Have you ever felt together alone
With God you're safe
You're always at home
www.God.calm means
You're never alone

WORDS AND MUSIC BY JENNIFER O'NEILL.
HANDSHAKE PRODUCTIONS.
USED BY PERMISSION

8

www.God.calm

Forgiving—The Key to Healing

The true value of an action or thought is . . . motive.
—J. O'N

FORGIVENESS HAS THREE PARTS: FIRST, WILLFULLY deciding to forgive, followed by canceling the debt of the offender, and then the surrender and release of the offender to God.

There are three Hebrew words meaning "to forgive." *Nasa* means to take away the barrier, to tear it down. That is the decision to forgive someone. *Kafar* means to cover the cost. Just as Christ covered our cost at Calvary, we are to cancel the debt of our offenders. *Salach* means to release, to let go of the person and leave things to God.

Forgive is defined in the dictionary as "to cease to cherish displeasure toward; pardon, excuse. To forego the penalty for, remit, as a debt."

Forgiveness is a big first step in our healing. As we begin peeling away the layers of unforgiveness and revealing ourselves while getting to the heart of the matter, let's ask these questions together, out loud. This is an important and thoughtful step in the journey toward healing. Let's just pretend I'm sitting next to you with a double bag of buttered popcorn and a hug as we consider these questions together:

1. Do I really want forgiveness to release my familiar resentments, excuses, hurts, baggage, anger, addictions, failures, ineffectuality, depression, loneliness, indiscretions, bad relationships, insecurities, and denial of the truth brought on by my unforgiveness?

2. Do I really want to be healed, or do I prefer to protect my familiar roles as victim, blamer, complainer, and guilty, emotionally damaged, limited, loveless, one-excuse-after-another woman?

3. Do I want to be the apple of Satan's eye as he lords life-robbing deception over me—or do I want to be a forgiven child of God, claiming His plan for my life in victory through the Holy Spirit?

4. Do I exhibit any behaviors that are sure signs of Satan's destructive use of our unforgiveness?

    • Do I hold resentment, hate, or ill will toward anyone, including myself?

    • Am I taking responsibility or passing the buck?

    • Do others pay for my bad memories, sad memories, and unresolved past?

    • Am I jealous when someone who hurt me is blessed?

PRACTICE WHAT WE PREACH

God said I first had to practice what I was given to preach. Yikes! I felt as if I was in the last painful contractions of a spiritual birth while stuck in a sweltering traffic jam, alone in my overheated car, with zero minutes left on my cell phone. Okay, okay, . . . breathe, breathe, breathe. Before I could even begin God's process of healing, I had to honestly review where my relationship was with God. I had to ask all those questions *again:* Did I really trust and have faith in God? Yes! Did I really believe He had the power and desire to reveal His truth to me, protect, empower, forgive, and heal me? Yes! Did I really believe He was going to do a great work in me and through me? Yes!

All right then. All I needed to do was to ask and believe I was about to receive!

> You want something but don't get it. You kill and covet, but you cannot have what you want. You quarrel and fight. You do not have, because you do not ask God. When you ask, you do not receive, because you ask with wrong motives, that you may spend what you get on your pleasures. (James 4:2–3)

Ask for the Holy Spirit to come into your heart and pray for you. Remember, God calls the Holy Spirit the Spirit of truth!

> But when he, the Spirit of truth, comes, he will guide you into all truth. He will not speak on his own; he will speak only what he hears, and he will tell you what is yet to come. (John 16:13)

I prayed out loud:

Dear Father God,

You have known my hurts and my heart since I was a little girl. You know everything that has happened to me and everything that I've done to others and to myself. *Everything!* You know why I don't want to remember . . . why it hurts so much that I can't even breathe sometimes. You know how angry I am, how ashamed and afraid I feel. I'm so tired of hurting and hating, acting badly and not knowing why. You promise I can curl up in Jesus' arms and that He'll protect me from everything. I feel so small right now . . . but I love and trust You, Father God. I love Jesus. I love the Holy Spirit with all my heart.

God, You have never lied to me, and I believe You love me, by Jesus' intercession, just the way I am, no matter what has happened. Through the power of the Holy Spirit, please show me all my pain and shame that I don't want to look at. I beg You to take me to every single memory, person and event, and horrible thing I've done, horrible things people have done to me that I don't think I can forgive, even those things that hurt so much I've kept them in dark, secret places. I don't want to go there alone, I don't want to remember by myself, but I'm asking the Holy Spirit to give me the words and lead me to everything that God wants me to see. And not just my past, but the things that I'm facing today. By His power, I can forgive everyone and everything . . . I can forgive me! Then God, You promise to forgive me and not even remember! I will finally be free and healed. I want that, Father . . . I ask and pray that now, please! In Jesus' name.

In the same way, the Spirit helps us in our weakness. We do not know what we ought to pray for, but the Spirit himself intercedes for us with groans that words cannot express. And he who searches our hearts knows the mind of the Spirit, because the Spirit intercedes for the saints in accordance with God's will. (Romans 8:26–27)

Jesus turned and saw her. "Take heart, daughter," he said, "your faith has healed you." And the woman was healed from that moment. (Matthew 9:22)

ROSES IN WINTER

They say that memories give us the power to gather roses in winter. When dealing with bad memories, I not only have to remember my past, I have to relive it, repent of it, rebuke it in Jesus' name, forgive, receive forgiveness, and then release it by giving those negative memories back to Jesus! I have to meet my pain where and when it happened, smell, taste, and feel every detail, leave nothing unturned, describe and confess it all out loud! Hurts hold us to hurtful behaviors, and problems have exact origins and details that can no longer be ignored. It is my call. God gave me free will. It is my request. It is my prayer.

Then you will know the truth, and the truth will set you free. (John 8:32)

As I began to traverse the shadows of my past in the arms of Jesus with the Holy Spirit at the helm, I found that some of my deepest, most devastating areas of pain remained with the unforgiveness of hurts regarding my mom and dad and my daughter, Aimee. I recognized that the long-running discord between Aimee and me began well before the sexual abuse she suffered. There just seemed to be an overriding friction to our relationship as a whole. I had to start the journey of discovery by facing the love-versus-dominance competition issues with my own mother before I could even approach my dynamic with Aimee. The relationship between mothers and daughters as they move from one generation to the next is incredibly complex and profound, igniting a full range of emotions that often vacillate with the passage of time.

As I mentioned, I had my first two children before I "had myself," a surefire recipe for disaster in the area of mothering. How can an emotionally needy, damaged, insecure individual supply her children with emotional stability when she herself doesn't embrace it? You can't, plain and simple. When Aimee and Reis were children, I raised them as my parents had raised me, with no idea of how to break established patterns. Actually, I wasn't even aware of the void of "individual nurturing" I was handing down at the time. It wasn't that Aimee and Reis were not cared for. They had the best, from schooling to a beautiful home. It was a lack of emotional availability and personal deep-seated hurt and anger on my part that drew the deepest wounds. I realize now that I was still dealing with my unmet needs (very poorly, I might add), so I was intrinsically unable to meet some of theirs. At nineteen, I thought I was ready to be a mom, but I was sorely unprepared. Furthermore, as a child I didn't have an available father as, thankfully, my daughter did, and as an adult I didn't have a loving husband in balance as my mother did. Yes, I was the mother, but still the echo of my emptiness came in surround-sound, and I didn't have a clue as to what was wrong! None of these statements are meant as an excuse; they are facts of my life.

Although portrayed in radically different styles, Mom, Aimee, and I are all extremely dominant females in our own right. Even though there still remains a very rare rough patch mixed in with deep love and respect for one another, there has been great and abiding healing between my mother and me over the years (especially recently!). Aimee and I have also shared improvement in our relationship. Still, despite the fact that we sincerely come to one another out of true yearning, upon deeper soul-searching I found there are unresolved issues that continue to block a full breakthrough of the hurtful areas between us.

EMPOWERED BY THE SPIRIT

My daughter and my parents have told me that they respect my "faith" but do not share my beliefs. I pray that somehow they will recognize that the process God led me through in my healing has released and set me free of strongholds that robbed my relationships with them in the past. The steps are demanding and do not require anyone else's approval or agreement—and the end results are so liberating!

> We have not received the spirit of the world but the Spirit who is from God, that we may understand what God has freely given us. This is what we speak, not in words taught us by human wisdom but in words taught by the Spirit, expressing spiritual truths in spiritual words. The man without the Spirit does not accept the things that come from the Spirit of God, for they are foolishness to him, and he cannot understand them, because they are spiritually discerned. (1 Corinthians 2:12–14)

When dealing with unbelievers in any part of our healing, we must not allow any misunderstandings or "viewpoints" to stand in the way of God's process. God clearly states that unbelievers (those without the Spirit of God) cannot understand spiritual truths taught by the Spirit with spiritual words. Unbelievers speak the language of the world, so don't let them sidetrack you! God's healing process cannot be done without the power of the Holy Spirit. He has to empower us and lead us to the *true* places of negative strongholds, since there are always two sides to every shared experience, and memories are so often selective. If we rely on our own recall, by our human defense mechanisms, we will invariably argue, get stuck on details, or skip over the *root* causes and areas of pain that bind us. Stay in the Spirit, led by the Holy Spirit, not in the "world's" spirit. This is so very important!

Forgiveness and healing are not about who is right and who is wrong, they are about releasing so *we* can receive forgiveness and healing. *God* will take care of all the appropriate retribution. In my own journey I needed to deal with my feelings *at the time* of the hurtful events rather than later "handling" my hurts. To break the enemy's holds requires the truth . . . not ours, but God's!

There is a saying in Christian lingo, "Love the sinner, hate the sin," and that, in a nutshell, was where God took me in regard to my mother, my daughter, and myself. (In fact, it applies to *all* of us, since we're all sinners.) At various times there existed an unidentified, combative "something" that displayed its ugliness in uniquely different ways in the three of us. It always threatened, worried, and scared me, but it wasn't until the process of forgiveness brought me face-to-face with what that "something" was that I began to truly understand. I realized that what I really saw in each of us was the manifestation of the same haughty, demanding, angry, controlling, destructive, combative spirit that so often led to devastating hurts and conflicts (especially when alcohol was added to the mix). The issue was not where that ugly spirit was birthed—we all have our individual points of painful origin. The reality was that it existed, and it was powerful and damaging. If you're looking in the face of anger, deceit, or any kind of threatening or negative behavior from anyone, that ugly spirit is the enemy and needs to be challenged, plain and simple! This applies to everyone.

TAKING RESPONSIBILITY

How many of you have ever had a spiteful husband, friend, or family member try to hurt you with this arsenal of words: "You're just like your mother!" Boy, that is scathing—but why does it hurt us so much? Invariably there are things we see in ourselves that reflect our mothers in areas we're not too fond of. We would prefer to take all the good stuff from Mom but leave the rest in the dust, thank you very much! Instead, let's take responsibility for ourselves and stop pointing the finger at everyone else . . . including our mothers. Remember, we are all inevitably responsible for everything we think, say, and do no matter what or who influenced our path.

The Holy Spirit showed me in the Word of God exactly what was going on in my life and taught me to identify and respond to the carnage of those negative spirits and sin nature in a Biblical context:

> Then Peter took Him aside and began to rebuke Him, saying, "Far be it from You, Lord; this shall not happen to You!" But He turned and said to Peter, "Get behind Me, Satan! You are an offense to Me, for you are not mindful of the things of God, but the things of men." (Matthew 16:22–23 NKJV)

There it was in black and white; Jesus loved and adored Peter, but He rebuked his behavior, *not* Peter himself! Jesus knew that Peter was going to deny Him three times before the very next morning, and He told Peter so. That didn't mean, however, that the disciple didn't love Jesus (and wouldn't later give his life for his faith in Him).

The Holy Spirit showed me by the love of Jesus that we're not to be held or bound by unforgiveness through anger, resentment, or sadness. Instead, it is the negative, evil spirits that need to be rebuked! Again, that does not mean we aren't accountable for every single one of our actions and behaviors. It just means that we have the power through the Holy Spirit to repent of those adverse actions and behaviors, and to forgive so God will forgive, heal, and free us. Once more, it is our choice.

MAKING FORGIVENESS REAL: GOD WASN'T FINISHED WITH ME YET!

Whew! I took a very deep breath, and before I could turn around, the Holy Spirit moved me on to another one of my wrenching areas of unforgiveness. He took me to each and every man—every husband I'd married in hopes of his love—a love that was not there. Their attacks, schemes, anger, and accusations had alienated my heart. I had to revisit and release all my feelings of being unlovable and invisible. I had to release my rage for those times of being lied to, used, abused, disrespected, and torn down. Further, my pathetic use of others as I acted out my anger and pain repulsed me. How unworthy and disgusted that made me feel about myself (all over again) and about them! It hurt so much, and held me in the trap of fury, hate, and self-loathing. I had to release it *all* through the power of the Holy Spirit. I had to forgive, confess, repent, and receive God's forgiveness. Finally, I gave all those people, feelings, and places of pain back to Jesus in His name! Giving it all to Jesus meant that I was not the debtholder any longer. The release felt like the first few minutes after having a cast removed from a healed leg. Right off, I was weak and unstable without the familiar shoring up of anger and hurt, but finally I was literally "cast off," and I reveled in the victory and freedom!

About a year ago I did a documentary for Promise Keepers directed by Jim Hanon, an enormously talented, godly filmmaker. From that work evolved a piece titled "Writing Dad." In it, I am the interviewer, but I'm also a participant by way of sharing my relationship with my own dad as others do in the documentary. Jim asked me to write a few letters to my father as segues within the piece.

LETTER 1:

Dear Dad,

There are so many things I love and admire about you, but at the top of my list is your faithfulness to Mom. You've shown me, over your fifty-five years of marriage, that falling in love can mean forever. You're a man of integrity and commitment, both adoring and protecting Mom as a good husband, lover, and friend. Her sense of security as a woman is testimony to your unwavering affection for her.

LETTER 2:

Dear Dad,

Ever since I can remember, I just wished we could have spent some time together . . . alone. I know you loved me, but you and Mom were so close to each other, there didn't seem to be any room for anyone else. I grew up thinking there must be something wrong with me: I must be unlovable. Dad, the most important thing you could have given me was your time. I missed you so very much.

LETTER 3:

Dear Dad,

You know that when my husband sexually molested my daughter, I was totally devastated for her and for me. I wished I could have run to you and that you somehow could make it all better. I wanted to feel protected, and I wanted your granddaughter to feel protected. I know you felt our pain, but it seemed hard for you to express it.

LETTER 4:

Dear Dad,

All I ever wanted since I was a little girl was to be happily married and have a family of my own. I know now that deep-seated desire was based on a hope that my husband would treat me as wonderfully as you've always treated Mom. You were a real live war hero, bigger than life in so many ways, and Dad, maybe I should have known how hard it was going to be to find a husband to follow in your footsteps. I'm so proud that you're my dad.

LETTER 5:

Dear Dad,

Remember when I wrote you about that hole in my heart? And we finally had a good laugh about the fact that most of my life, my theme song was "Looking for Love in All the Wrong Places." I was so desperately unhappy and unfulfilled. But now that's all changed. I'm finally in touch with my heavenly Father's unconditional love, which, by the way, Dad, reminds me of the love I have for you. And as I write this letter to share my feelings with you, I am also praying to Him, because He is the author of love. I thank God you're my dad and I'll always be your little girl. Hugs and kisses!

I told my father about the "Writing Dad" project and asked if he would be willing to appear with me in the show. He said sure. I read him the little segue letters so he'd have a feel for the project. His eyes teared slightly, something I've only seen a few times before . . . when he would reminisce about the war. Of course, Dad always becomes very teary-eyed when he thinks of his bride, Rene. But this moment was mine, and I was so touched that it was my turn to be included in his obvious expression of love. He had always seemed so out of reach to me.

We had a wonderful conversation; wonderful because it was honest but not angry. I told him that all I ever wanted was to have a "date" with my dad once in a while, just some time alone with each other together. I said, "We've never had a pizza together, Dad, or gone to a movie. You've never taken a ride on my horses with me. And it's not just about me . . . You've never once thrown a ball to your grandsons, or great-grandsons." He just nodded (not with guilt) and stated, "Yup, I don't like to do those kinds of things. That's just me, Jen."

When the Holy Spirit took me to my places of unforgiveness with my dad, although the pain and hurt ran deep, the forgiveness came easily. First, because I've been forgiven of so much! Secondly, I didn't *need* to be affirmed by my father anymore to make me feel complete because, since I had come to Christ, that hole in my heart was filled by my Father in heaven. All the past hurts of absenteeism, criticism, and teasing from my father (again, exacerbated by drinking) was his sin that I could now separate from the wonderful man I call Dad. I now can love him just the way he is, and I can love me just the way I am, because that's just the way God loves us!

For the shot at the end of the show, the director wanted Dad and me to walk down the driveway. We put our arms around each other and I kissed my father like a little girl. It was an awe-some moment as well as a beautiful visual, and when we walked back to the crew, Dad said to Jim, "You know, I've never done that before." Jim responded, "You've never been filmed before?" "No,"—Dad teared up again—"I've never taken a little walk with my daughter alone before." Jim beamed, "Well, maybe some dads that see this documentary will invite their daughters to go on a walk with them."

> I pray also that the eyes of your heart may be enlightened in order that you may know the hope to which he has called you, the riches of his glorious inheritance in the saints, and his incomparably great power for us who believe. That power is like the working of his mighty strength. (Ephesians 1:18–19)

The very last night of working on this book, I came home after a meeting with the publisher. As I arrived, the phone rang. It was my older son, Reis, calling from the West Coast to "catch up." Wow, what a gift that was for me. He said that he and his fiancée were going to come back to Nashville for about six months to "regroup and make plans." Reis and I talked openly about life goals, fears, school, work, and a general direction for his future. Our conversation was an answer to prayer, since Reis had kept to himself for the most part over the last year. Without the benefit of a strong male figure in his life, Reis hasn't had the easiest passage into manhood. Nonetheless, he's an extraordinarily talented artist with a unique ability to communicate with others of all ages, easily offering his heart and his wonderful sense of humor to all. I'm so proud to be his mom! We made plans for him and his brother, Cooper, to spend time together (they both truly love and miss each other). My heart sang!

I immediately banged on Mom and Dad's door to tell them I had heard from Reis and that he sent his love. Merve was working, so just the three of us sat and yakked for a good long while about the family, this book, and the fact that I would be finishing it that night . . . and then, something extraordinary happened! First God had blessed me with a call from my son and then He gave me the most amazing outpouring of tenderness and love from my parents that I had ever experienced. They expressed, without reservations, unilateral interest and support of this book and of me. Their pride and best wishes absolutely filled me with joy and affirmation. I told them that moment felt as though every missed date, misunderstanding, missed horse show, missed outing, missed pizza, missed anything I could think of, was suddenly filled in and accounted for. It was then, when I was so full of God's love and I wasn't screaming and crying for theirs, that my parents showed up with bells on! There are no words to describe the miraculous mending and filling of God's forgiveness and healing that occurred that night. The next morning these two letters were outside my bedroom door:

Dearest Jennifer,

When you were nine years old you hit the heights of my affection for you. But the process has never stopped and it never will. Today at your wonderful age of 53, a new wave of love and admiration keeps flowing from you. It strikes me, and everyone else around you. You have a built-in needle that invariably points true north on any moral compass. I love you.

Dad

prayed together for our husbands. We prayed for each other's missions and the mission God brought us together for. We read
Scriptures to ourselves and each other. The healings started to
happen just when they were needed. I reached to my heart to find
the forgiveness for my husband, my mother, my grandmother, my
school years of pain, the man who wrongfully touched me as a
child, my medical problems, jealousy, the man who killed my
father, alcoholism in my family, and more. I knew I had to start
with a clean slate if I were to do the next stage of God's mission
for me to help rid these single mothers and extended families of
this same pain that held me back for years by helping them go
through the process of forgiveness and healing.

After reading Jennifer's new book, *From Fallen to Forgiven*,
my life seemed to change even more for the better. I felt a closure,
forgiveness, and a clear direction within myself I have never felt
before. It was like after reading Jennifer's book all the i's in my
life are now dotted and complete. By the way, for two nights in a
row my husband has had the same dream—that he has his old
Donna back. I'm back, Spirit-filled and ready to serve the Lord!

*Father God, thank You for Donna. She is such a faithful, bold
sister in Christ! I ask Your continued blessings over her and her
family, and lead us clearly in our work together in Your glory. In
Jesus' name.*

LAURA'S STORY

*I met Laura at the very first Fallen to Forgiven seminar in Katy,
Texas. I was immediately taken with her love for the Lord, her
openness, and her tenacity. I'm sure I'll see her again and we'll
both be able to share great victories in Christ!*

Thanks so much for the time we spent on Monday morning. I've been wanting to write to you. For a couple of days—between motherhood, payroll, and quarterly taxes, this is the first time I've had a chance to sit down—and even now, I feel like I'm cheating. I'm here with three kids and no housekeeper, so if my thoughts seem disjointed . . .

In response to your question of how the healing workshop affected me—the most amazing thing happened! I really hope I can effectively put this into words.

I didn't start to put things together until Monday afternoon, more Tuesday, and more today. On Sunday, after church and lunch and a nap, I walked to the back of our property (with your book coincidentally) and sat lazily on our bench swing and read. Having moments like that to myself are rare, so when I looked up and saw Izzie (my three-year-old) making her way across the backyard toward me, I unconsciously anticipated a wave of tenseness and disappointment—which didn't come. It wasn't a huge surprise to me that I felt a peaceful welcoming toward Izzie—she's a cuddly, quiet, happy child. For me, getting interrupted by Izzie represents a fifty/fifty chance of feeling even mildly irritated.

A few minutes after she made herself quietly comfortable on the swing, I looked up and saw Winnie (six years old) cutting the same path toward me. Again I braced myself for a secret hardening in my heart—almost guaranteed by an interruption from Winnie. Winnie is a joyful, bright, beautiful, chatty, high-energy child, who demands almost nonstop interaction and creates nonstop noise. I hold myself in secret contempt for the irritation she stimulates in my spirit.

Guess what? That pinch never grabbed my heart! It was kind of like stubbing my toe and bracing myself for a guaranteed wave of pain that amazingly never crested—never even threatened to swell. Just a perfectly placid pool in my heart, and I peacefully welcomed this incredible little nymphlike creature of God's into my quiet space—to be who she was, whatever she wanted.

It was a very new feeling for me. Absent was the familiar feeling of subdued resentment over having my precious alone-time stolen from me. It is a hard feeling to fully describe; it almost feels like the beginning of rage. Then I never quite "juice back up" before someone tries to suck what little I have out of me, and Winnie is the most voracious of the suckers.

There have been several other situations over the past four days that would have been perfect opportunities for that hateful feeling to swell up in me. But it hasn't happened. Noticing that is what called my attention to the fact that something has changed. And the only thing I can attribute it to is the prayer you said over us.

I'm wondering if there is some generational sin connected to my feelings of resentment and being overwhelmed in relation to my kids. My mother used to be pretty open about expressing her overwhelmedness as a mother, although I never heard her express resentment. But then, knowing Mom as I do, it would make more sense that she would feel terrible about feeling that way and, like me, would not say it. I remember stories that make me think that Mom's mother could easily have had the same feelings. I also know that my great-grandmother walked out on her two daughters. And that there was some kind of schism between my great-great-grandmother and her daughter.

I would have never thought that this feeling I had was generational sin. But in tracking it through my mother's family and having been covered by your prayer . . . I can only guess that it is exactly that. I feel a peace I have not felt in years. I have a gentleness toward my children, even when I'm angry, that was so much a part of who I was years ago. I am laughing like I used to, which is a lot.

Another thing that has been very freeing, and I'm sure has contributed to my change of spirit, has to do with your discussion on prayer for forgiveness. I didn't feel the need or desire to succumb to emotionalism, but I did feel pain. I wanted to mentally absorb your words, and at the same time I realized my pain must be an indication that I had work to do in the area of forgiveness.

I have spent the days since your workshop mentally defaulting into meditative thought about forgiveness and especially your comment that we don't have to continue to do business with someone we have forgiven. That was an affirmation of a recent epiphany as well as a springboard for another. I also realize that just because I have forgiven someone, I don't have to force myself into eradicating the pain before the pain has completed its purpose. In other words, I don't have to stop hurting for the forgiveness to be authentic! The sword of the Spirit once again divided what I thought was a singular issue into two unrelated parts. That understanding freed me up to *fluidly* forgive a lot of people and clean out numerous spiritual nooks and crannies.

I feel so light I could fly . . . my husband just came to the doorway to tell me he had poured a bath for me with salts and candles . . . Gee, I wonder what he wants? Actually, he's been really sweet to me for an extended period of time. Could it be that God is answering prayer? This is much more than I asked for. We serve an awesome Papa!

Father God, whenever You manifest Your promises in our lives we are humbled in thanksgiving and praise. Thank You, Lord, for Your hand on Laura, and may Your mercy and favor shine like a beacon through her. In Jesus' name.

MELISSA'S STORY

I was speaking with Cindy of Bethlehem Farms (she prepared the Jesus Love Letter in chapter four), and she told me of an amazing story of healing she had just witnessed with a woman named Melissa. What confirmation from God! I asked if Melissa would mind sharing her story with you.

It wasn't until my current age of forty-four that the items holding me back from forgiveness became explosive in my life; almost costing me my job of eighteen years, costing me several friendships that were held dear, and creating within a deep desire to end my life. I was no longer able to mask my feelings, to be the cool, level-headed, compassionate person that I had always led others to believe I was. The anger in my life that was so deeply and so carefully stuffed down within my being became explosive, erupting in a volcanic action toward my supervisor. Overnight, the "passion" left the compassion, leaving anger, hate, bitterness, guilt, shame, lack of self-worth, and many other deep-set feelings bubbling to the surface in self-destructive action that could not be extinguished.

I had learned at a very early age by the abusive hands of my father to keep my true emotions hidden. The tears that I so desperately wished to cry I stuffed deep within my soul. If I let them out it was an excuse for him to provide comfort in a very inappropriate way. By the age of five I knew that my father would always be the one to tuck me in at night, every night without fail. I wanted to bear the pain of his hands only once a day, so I kept my emotions quiet.

The age of seven led to cultic ceremonies and rituals, and a lot of confusion. Where was God when I called out in pain? He did not answer.

Added to pain were now anger and disillusionment. The feelings of bitterness and lack of self-worth stepped in at the age of thirteen. An abortion took place at the hands of a "back-closet doctor." The child within was not male, therefore unnecessary for the purpose of the cult, and was to be destroyed. (I would never be able to bear children due to the damage that was done.) The abuse continued far into adulthood. A loaded gun became a great intimidation. After my father passed away unexpectedly, I thought I had found the freedom I craved and all would be well within my life. Little did I know the problems were just beginning with this event. The feelings I stuffed down so deep that I thought they would never surface were manifesting themselves, however subtly.

I felt a great need to be accepted, so the lying started. For so many years I had not been "good enough," so I invented the perfect life, living in lies. I became a workaholic, needing to be perfect in every way. I accepted Christ into my life. I was deathly afraid of hugs or touch, so when one became close to me I pushed him or her away by any means possible.

Only when I was with my horse did I find true solace. Having been an abuse case, Blackstone and I grew out of our abuse together, learning unconditional love for each other in the process. My life became tolerable because of the love for my horse and soon my life was on the mend again, or so I thought. I was still a very lonely person, not letting people near. I had, however, the love of my horse, and that was all that mattered. Once again, how wrong I was.

My horse, the love of my life, was struck with a ravaging bacterial infection that settled into his eyes. I was told that he would be blind within a month. We did everything we could for "my boy," yet nothing worked. I became angry with God, feeling that this was punishment for my past. There might be something in prayer. I was angry with God, but there were others who were not. I contacted Cindy of Bethlehem Farms and asked for prayers for my horse. As Blackstone's treatments continued, so did my correspondence with Cindy. As the prayer warriors for Bethlehem Farms continued to uphold my horse, Cindy, in a very loving, non-threatening way, started ministering to my wounded soul.

Even as the healing progressed in my horse and I was seeing the results of powerful prayer, I was falling into deeper and deeper despair. The feelings of the past were coming to an eruptive state. I could not force them down any longer, and the explosion came at work. That day, I'm sure by the grace of God, my job was spared. It was not the anger that came forth, but a deep hatred within my eyes that frightened my supervisor that day. I was immediately placed into counseling. It was then I realized that I needed to make some major decisions in my life. I was so very tired of fighting the feelings, tired of trying to hide who I really was, tired of living. I fell into a deep clinical depression and wanted desperately to end my life. I also knew at that point Christ was in my life, but not *within* my life. Counseling and medication were helping to control the problem, but were not getting to the root issues. I wanted something more but was not sure where to turn.

Cindy told me about Tommy, a counselor who had offered his services to Bethlehem Farms' ministry. He dealt with deep-rooted issues and the healing of those issues through a gentle approach using prayer. It took a couple of weeks for me to make contact with him. At this point in time I had grown to trust Cindy with my thoughts and feelings, but to open up to someone else, to become vulnerable once again, I just wasn't sure I trusted that much. I did finally make contact. Plans were made and dates finalized to meet with Tommy. Terror became a great part of my life. Phone conversations kept me on track, but I began fighting this trip with all my being.

As Cindy arrived where I was staying, she found me hugging a tree and in tears. What had I gotten myself into? I did not want to be there. I did not want to go through this counseling; I was terrified. The day progressed and my fears lessened. I began to release, Tommy never pushing, always praying and gently leading me to a healing I never thought possible.

Release did not come until forgiveness had taken place within my heart. I did need to forgive. Forgive my father, my family, myself, the doctor who performed the abortion, and so many others. Until forgiveness, *true forgiveness,* was in place, I was not free of my past demons and haunts. Healing had become complete, and for the first time I could close my eyes and see myself within the embrace of Jesus. I left with a song on my lips, my feet dancing in joy and my heart filled to overflowing.

I'm sorry I lost half of my life to my emotions, and I pray that others may find the true key to healing before they lose so much of life! How good forgiveness feels!

Thank You, Lord, for the grace and healing You have shown Melissa, and we pray that Your hand remains on her for Your full will and purpose in this loving sister's life! In Jesus' mighty name.

Trisha's Story

I saw you on TBN today and was pleasantly shocked to find out you were now a Christian. You completely held my attention as you were giving your testimony and sharing about your new book. You don't know how much I related to your life and how many years it took me as a Christian to ever feel cleansed from all the sinning I had gotten into after I accepted the Lord as my Savior. My marriage ended in a divorce, scattering my family. Then I remarried before I had even dealt with my past! I have gone through so much sorrow and self-inflicted pain, which God said I would experience (as we reap what we sow), but I just need to say that I finally did do what you were talking about on television, and that was to go to all those places where I had been hurt. I also went to all those people whom I had hurt and truly repented, sincerely asked for forgiveness. I have truly prayed for the Lord to use me to help other "lost" Christians who think they are of no value in God's plan because they have messed up their lives so badly. When I first became saved I must have thought that I would be "perfect" from then on or something. But years of struggling due to ignorance of what God is truly about left me tossed to and fro, as James talks about in the Word.

Jennifer, we really don't know the truth sometimes! We truly need the older ones teaching the younger ones and giving real-life stories and true testimonies, and that's why I am writing to you—to thank God for your transparency and your genuine care, love, and concern for the lost, and the body of Christ. Please continue to speak the whole counsel of God. Please never water down the truth. Our Great and Mighty God needs those like you to reach out in places most don't experience. Be faithful to Him, Jennifer, not to man and his opinion. Once again, thank you for sharing your life with us.

Spiritual Map for the Journey

God's Healing Process and Inspiration

A. GOD'S HEALING PROCESS

For review of stepping through from unforgiveness to healing and wholeness, we must have at least one or more trusted persons present and participating in our verbal journey from "Fallen to Forgiven," which will bring release and healing. Your partner(s) in the process must be a *believing Christian,* be it a counselor, a sister in Christ, a husband, a friend, or an acquaintance. Be sure that person's faith is mature, and that he or she is knowledgeable in the Word and has an abiding prayer power . . . and no personal agenda. And again, *you are not alone!*

1. Make sure you have all your Scripture references readily available. Together, pray for the presence, power, and *revealing* of the Holy Spirit, the covering forgiveness of the blood and mercy of Jesus Christ, and the unconditional love of God our Father to enter our places of pain and unforgiveness. A Christian partner(s) should be prepared at any needed time to step in with powerful intercessory prayers

and leadings on behalf of the one going through God's process of forgiveness!

2. Look your Christian partner(s) in the eye and rebuke Satan *out loud*—put him on notice and boldly claim the intent and victory of what will follow in your process of healing and your desire to be healed.

3. Make sure that now you are choosing to forgive and heal. Also know that God (through the power of the Holy Spirit) requires you to describe and reexperience *out loud* all thoughts and actions of past painful events as the Holy Spirit determines the truth from the lies that have led to bondage. Now you must personally identify your perpetrator(s) and admit how the hurtful events made you feel— dirty, bad, a participant, anger, shame, everything that has been haunting you and playing on your lifelong negative tape. Then you must forgive, and release from the heart, those who have harmed you! *But* maybe *we* were the perpetrator. What then? Same process! Don't miss anything, anyone, any detail, or any experience as you release each one of these people or actions (or yourself) one at a time through your forgiveness. Truthfully relive to truly live again; admit, repent, rebuke, and *get bold* about reclaiming what has been lost to you by your own hand or others.

4. Put the enemy on notice—*out loud*—that the "robbing fest" is *over*! Tell him that he *must leave,* in the name of Jesus.

5. Now give all your stolen moments, numbed feelings, lost identity, and lost relationships back to Jesus. He will recall every area of your past hurts and pain back to Himself as restored. He'll take it all; just ask Him, "Please, in the power of the Holy Spirit," and it is done! Out loud—kick

Satan out in the name of Jesus! Remember, this is a process and some unforgiveness takes longer to get to, but eventually you will find your way to freedom through the power of the Holy Spirit. Don't give up! (Christian partner[s] may have to intervene with compassionate strength and powerful prayer.)

6. Look your Christian partner(s) in the eye, and once again verbally confirm your rebuke of the enemy and state that God loves you—that you have forgiven from your heart, and that you are worthy of His love and of your healing, acceptance, and release through the blood of Christ. Tell your partner the area of your life that God has just taken back. Note that this period of confession, recognition, reliving, announcing, rebuking, repenting, and reclaiming may very well require some "screaming" energetic rebuke . . . or God's grace may come as quietly as the sweetest dream you've ever had. Either way or in between, get at it with unwavering conviction that you are about to be released through your unforgiveness into God's forgiveness and the very healing, restoration, and jump-start of your soul and future in Christ.

7. Praise God for your release and healing, and seal it with a prayer covering.

8. As soon as possible after your process, list each step through releasing your unforgiveness and all areas of forgiveness and healing. Own that victory daily, so as not to be robbed by the enemy of what God has worked in your life.

9. Live your victories confidently in Christ as a beacon of hope for others and in the confidence that comes only from God!

B. CHECKLIST FOR CHRISTIAN GROWTH

I wanted to share with you my checklist for Christian growth that has been so helpful for me. Hey, if I take my car in for alignment, why shouldn't I at least do the same for myself?

1. Are we increasingly aware of our sinful nature and weaknesses?

2. Is our response to sin quick, followed by genuine confession and repentance?

3. As our spiritual battles become more fierce, do we *rejoice* in all our circumstances?

4. Do we regard trials and temptations as opportunities for growth, and enjoy God's peace beyond understanding?

5. Do we view service to Him as the highest honor, not a burden? All that we do, do we do it for His glory?

6. Do we embrace discipline and lessons that come our way as gifts from God, and are we thankful? Are we led not by sight, but by faith?

7. Do we sense our faith is growing stronger? Have we become better witnesses for Him as a result?

8. Do we desire to spend more time in genuine praise and worship as godly submission and humility are truly understood as empowerment, not weakness?

9. Is our desire to obey Him becoming more intense, and sin less and less attractive to us? As we turn from *selfish* to *selfless*, are we more keenly aware when we grieve the Holy Spirit?

10. Are we eager to share with others what Christ is doing in our lives and what Christ longs to do in theirs?

11. Do we experience an increasing awareness of His presence and of how to be in continual prayer? Are we able to hear the whisperings of the Holy Spirit?

12. Do we jealously guard our private time of Bible reading and prayer, preferring to spend time with Him above all others?

13. Do all of our relationships reflect our increasingly intimate relationship with God and flourish on Biblical truths?

14. Are we quick to obey God in *all* things?

Please, don't be complacent; be challenged. Denied experiences only become more powerful through their rerouted expressions of illness, aging, anger, and addictions in our lives. No more cover-up! And remember, *you are not alone!*

C. Promises from the Word

> I have hidden your word in my heart
> that I might not sin against you.
> —Psalm 119:11

Brokenheartedness

The sacrifices of God are a broken spirit; a broken and contrite heart, O God, you will not despise. (Psalm 51:17)

The LORD is close to the brokenhearted and saves those who are crushed in spirit. (Psalm 34:18)

Condemnation

Therefore, there is now no condemnation for those who are in Christ Jesus. (Romans 8:1)

This then is how we know that we belong to the truth, and how we set our hearts at rest in his presence whenever our hearts condemn us. For God is greater than our hearts, and he knows everything. (1 John 3:19–20)

But now he has reconciled you by Christ's physical body through death to present you holy in his sight, without blemish and free from accusation. (Colossians 1:22)

CONFESSION

Therefore confess your sins to each other and pray for each other so that you may be healed. The prayer of a righteous man is powerful and effective. (James 5:16)

FAITH

We live by faith, not by sight. (2 Corinthians 5:7)

In him and through faith in him we may approach God with freedom and confidence. (Ephesians 3:12)

And without faith it is impossible to please God, because anyone who comes to him must believe that he exists and that he rewards those who earnestly seek him. (Hebrews 11:6)

Now faith is being sure of what we hope for and certain of what we do not see. (Hebrews 11:1)

It is written: "I believed; therefore I have spoken." With that same spirit of faith we also believe and therefore speak. (2 Corinthians 4:13)

If you have faith as small as a mustard seed, you can say to this mountain, "Move from here to there" and it will move. Nothing will be impossible for you. (Matthew 17:20–21)

Everything is possible for him who believes. (Mark 9:23)

Consequently, faith comes from hearing the message, and the message is heard through the word of Christ. (Romans 10:17)

FORGIVENESS

For if you forgive men when they sin against you, your heavenly Father will also forgive you. But if you do not forgive men their sins, your Father will not forgive your sins. (Matthew 6:14–15)

And when you stand praying, if you hold anything against anyone, forgive him, so that your Father in heaven may forgive you your sins. (Mark 11:25–26)

Be kind and compassionate to one another, forgiving each other, just as in Christ God forgave you. (Ephesians 4:32)

Bear with each other and forgive whatever grievances you may have against one another. Forgive as the Lord forgave you. (Colossians 3:13)

If we confess our sins, he is faithful and just and will forgive us our sins and purify us from all unrighteousness. (1 John 1:9)

For as high as the heavens are above the earth, so great is his love for those who fear him; as far as the east is from the west, so far has he removed our transgressions from us. (Psalm 103:11–12)

Repent, then, and turn to God, so that your sins may be wiped out, that times of refreshing may come from the Lord. (Acts 3:19)

Who is a God like you, who pardons sin and forgives the transgression of the remnant of his inheritance? You do not stay angry forever but delight to show mercy. You will again have compassion on us; you will tread our sins underfoot and hurl all our iniquities into the depths of the sea. (Micah 7:18–19)

FRIENDSHIP

A friend loves at all times. (Proverbs 17:17)

Wounds from a friend can be trusted, but an enemy multiplies kisses. (Proverbs 27:6)

A man of many companions may come to ruin, but there is a friend who sticks closer than a brother. (Proverbs 18:24)

Two are better than one, because they have a good return for their work: If one falls down, his friend can help him up. But pity the man who falls and has no one to help him up! Also, if two lie down together, they will keep warm. But how can one keep warm alone? Though one may be overpowered, two can defend themselves. A cord of three strands is not quickly broken. (Ecclesiastes 4:9–12)

GENERATIONAL SIN

It is for freedom that Christ has set us free. Stand firm, then, and do not let yourselves be burdened again by a yoke of slavery. (Galatians 5:1)

They will rebuild the ancient ruins and restore the places long devastated; they will renew the ruined cities that have been devastated for generations. (Isaiah 61:4)

The boundary lines have fallen for me in pleasant places; surely I have a delightful inheritance. (Psalm 16:6)

Then you will know the truth, and the truth will set you free. (John 8:32)

Yet you ask, "Why does the son not share the guilt of his father?" Since the son has done what is just and right and has been careful to keep all my decrees, he will surely live. (Ezekiel 18:19)

Brothers, I do not consider myself yet to have taken hold of it. But one thing I do: Forgetting what is behind and straining toward what is ahead. (Philippians 3:13)

I, the LORD your God, am a jealous God, punishing the children for the sin of the fathers to the third and fourth generation of those who hate me, but showing love to a thousand [generations] of those who love me and keep my commandments. (Exodus 20:5–6)

GOD'S CHARACTER

Ah, Sovereign LORD, you have made the heavens and the earth by your great power and outstretched arm. Nothing is too hard for you. (Jeremiah 32:17)

Trust in him at all times, O people; pour out your hearts to him, for God is our refuge. (Psalm 62:8)

Be still, and know that I am God. (Psalm 46:10)

Cast all your anxiety on him because he cares for you. (1 Peter 5:7)

For God is not a God of disorder but of peace. (1 Corinthians 14:33)

Righteous are you, O LORD, and your laws are right. (Psalm 119:137)

He is the Rock, his works are perfect, and all his ways are just. A faithful God who does no wrong, upright and just is he. (Deuteronomy 32:4)

Whoever does not love does not know God, because God is love. (1 John 4:8)

O LORD, you have searched me and you know me. You know when I sit and when I rise; you perceive my thoughts from afar. You discern my going out and my lying down; you are familiar with all my ways. Before a word is on my tongue you know it completely, O LORD. You hem me in—behind and before; you have laid your hand upon me. Such knowledge is too wonderful for me, too lofty for me to attain. (Psalm 139:1–6)

I know that you can do all things; no plan of yours can be thwarted. (Job 42:2)

Into your hands I commit my spirit; redeem me, O LORD, the God of truth. (Psalm 31:5)

I the LORD do not change. (Malachi 3:6)

May the God who gives endurance and encouragement give you a spirit of unity among yourselves as you follow Christ Jesus. (Romans 15:5)

God . . . does not lie. (Titus 1:2)

GOD'S PROTECTION

But you are a shield around me, O LORD; you bestow glory on me and lift up my head. (Psalm 3:3)

I will lie down and sleep in peace, for you alone, O LORD, make me dwell in safety. (Psalm 4:8)

The angel of the LORD encamps around those who fear him, and he delivers them. (Psalm 34:7)

He who dwells in the shelter of the Most High will rest in the shadow of the Almighty. (Psalm 91:1)

But the Lord is faithful, and he will strengthen and protect you from the evil one. (2 Thessalonians 3:3)

My prayer is . . . that you protect them from the evil one. (John 17:15)

He guards the course of the just and protects the way of his faithful ones. (Proverbs 2:8)

The LORD is my light and my salvation—whom shall I fear? The LORD is the stronghold of my life—of whom shall I be afraid? (Psalm 27:1)

When you lie down, you will not be afraid; when you lie down, your sleep will be sweet. Have no fear of sudden disaster or of the ruin that overtakes the wicked, for the LORD will be your confidence and will keep your foot from being snared. (Proverbs 3:24–26)

GOD'S VIEW OF ME

What if some did not have faith? Will their lack of faith nullify God's faithfulness? Not at all! (Romans 3:3–4)

If we are faithless, he will remain faithful, for he cannot disown himself. (2 Timothy 2:13)

For the LORD takes delight in his people; he crowns the humble with salvation. (Psalm 149:4)

Who is a God like you, who pardons sin and forgives the transgression of the remnant of his inheritance? You do not stay angry forever but delight to show mercy. (Micah 7:18)

Because of the LORD's great love we are not consumed, for his compassions never fail. They are new every morning; great is your faithfulness. (Lamentations 3:22–23)

As a father has compassion on his children, so the LORD has compassion on those who fear him. (Psalm 103:13)

The LORD did not set his affection on you and choose you because you were more numerous than other peoples, for you were the fewest of all peoples. But it was because the LORD loved you and kept the oath he swore to your forefathers that he brought you out with a mighty hand and redeemed you from the land of slavery, from the power of Pharaoh king of Egypt. Know therefore that the LORD your God is God; he is the faithful God, keeping his covenant of love to a thousand generations of those who love him and keep his commands. (Deuteronomy 7:7–9)

He has taken me to the banquet hall, and his banner over me is love. (Song of Songs 2:4)

To him who is able to keep you from falling and to present you before his glorious presence without fault and with great joy. (Jude 24)

For men are not cast off by the Lord forever. Though he brings grief, he will show compassion, so great is his unfailing love. For he does not willingly bring affliction or grief to the children of men. (Lamentations 3:31–33)

For the LORD God is a sun and shield; the LORD bestows favor and honor; no good thing does he withhold from those whose walk is blameless. (Psalm 84:11)

Can a mother forget the baby at her breast and have no compassion on the child she has borne? Though she may forget, I will not forget you! See, I have engraved you on the palms of my hands; your walls are ever before me. (Isaiah 49:15–16)

Praise the LORD, O my soul, and forget not all his benefits—who forgives all your sins and heals all your diseases, who redeems your life from the pit and crowns you with love and compassion, who satisfies your desires with good things so that your youth is renewed like the eagle's. The LORD works righteousness and justice for all the oppressed. (Psalm 103:2–6)

The thief comes only to steal and kill and destroy; I have come that they may have life, and have it to the full. (John 10:10)

I praise you because I am fearfully and wonderfully made; your works are wonderful, I know that full well. (Psalm 139:14)

Never will I leave you; never will I forsake you. (Hebrews 13:5)

And we know that in all things God works for the good of those who love him, who have been called according to his purpose. (Romans 8:28)

I pray that out of his glorious riches he may strengthen you with power through his Spirit in your inner being, so that Christ may dwell in your hearts through faith. And I pray that you, being rooted and established in love, may have power, together with all the saints, to grasp how wide and long and high and deep is the love of Christ, and to know this love that surpasses knowledge—that you may be filled to the measure of all the fullness of God. Now to him who is able to do immeasurably more than all we ask or imagine, according to his power that is at work within us, to him be glory in the church and in Christ Jesus throughout all generations, for ever and ever! Amen. (Ephesians 3:16–21)

If God is for us, who can be against us? (Romans 8:31)

But thanks be to God, who always leads us in triumphal procession in Christ and through us spreads everywhere the fragrance of the knowledge of him. (2 Corinthians 2:14)

The LORD appeared to us in the past, saying: "I have loved you with an everlasting love; I have drawn you with lovingkindness." (Jeremiah 31:3)

GRACE

For I will forgive their wickedness and will remember their sins no more. (Jeremiah 31:34)

From the fullness of his grace we have all received one blessing after another. (John 1:16)

For sin shall not be your master, because you are not under law, but under grace. (Romans 6:14)

And God is able to make all grace abound to you, so that in all things at all times, having all that you need, you will abound in every good work. (2 Corinthians 9:8)

But he said to me, "My grace is sufficient for you, for my power is made perfect in weakness." Therefore I will boast all the more gladly about my weaknesses, so that Christ's power may rest on me. (2 Corinthians 12:9)

Grace and peace be yours in abundance through the knowledge of God and of Jesus our Lord. (2 Peter 1:2)

HEALING, RESTORATION, AND RELEASE

But he was pierced for our transgressions, he was crushed for our iniquities; the punishment that brought us peace was upon him, and by his wounds we are healed. (Isaiah 53:5)

He himself bore our sins in his body on the tree, so that we might die to sins and live for righteousness; by his wounds you have been healed. (1 Peter 2:24)

Jesus turned and saw her. "Take heart, daughter," he said, "your faith has healed you." And the woman was healed from that moment. (Matthew 9:22)

But I will restore you to health and heal your wounds," declares the LORD. (Jeremiah 30:17)

I have loved you with an everlasting love; I have drawn you with loving-kindness. I will build you up again and you will be rebuilt. (Jeremiah 31:3–4)

I will give them an undivided heart and put a new spirit in them; I will remove from them their heart of stone and give them a heart of flesh. (Ezekiel 11:19)

This is the word that came to Jeremiah from the LORD: "Go down to the potter's house, and there I will give you my message." So I went down to the potter's house, and I saw him working at the wheel. But the pot he was shaping from the clay was marred in his hands; so the potter formed it into another pot, shaping it as seemed best to him. Then the word of the LORD came to me: "O house of Israel, can I not do with you as this potter does?" declares the LORD. "Like clay in the hand of the potter, so are you in my hand, O house of Israel." (Jeremiah 18:1–6)

It is for freedom that Christ has set us free. (Galatians 5:1)

I pray also that the eyes of your heart may be enlightened in order that you may know the hope to which he has called you, the riches of his glorious inheritance in the saints, and his incomparably great power for us who believe. (Ephesians 1:18–19)

And the God of all grace, who called you to his eternal glory in Christ, after you have suffered a little while, will himself restore you and make you strong, firm and steadfast. (1 Peter 5:10)

The Spirit of the Sovereign LORD is on me, because the LORD has anointed me to preach good news to the poor. He has sent me to bind up the brokenhearted, to proclaim freedom for the captives and release from darkness for the prisoners, to proclaim the year of the LORD's favor and the day of vengeance of our God, to comfort all who mourn, and provide for those who grieve in Zion— to bestow on them a crown of beauty instead of ashes, the oil of gladness instead of mourning, and a garment of praise instead of a spirit of despair. They will be called oaks of righteousness, a planting of the LORD for the display of his splendor. They will rebuild the ancient ruins and restore the places long devastated;

they will renew the ruined cities that have been devastated for generations. (Isaiah 61:1–4)

LEADING OF THE HOLY SPIRIT

But when he, the Spirit of truth, comes, he will guide you into all truth. He will not speak on his own; he will speak only what he hears, and he will tell you what is yet to come. He will bring glory to me by taking from what is mine and making it known to you. (John 16:13–14)

Now the Lord is the Spirit, and where the Spirit of the Lord is, there is freedom. (2 Corinthians 3:17)

PRAYER

Ask and it will be given to you; seek and you will find; knock and the door will be opened to you. For everyone who asks receives; he who seeks finds; and to him who knocks, the door will be opened. Which of you, if his son asks for bread, will give him a stone? Or if he asks for a fish, will give him a snake? If you, then, though you are evil, know how to give good gifts to your children, how much more will your Father in heaven give good gifts to those who ask him! (Matthew 7:7–11)

Again, I tell you that if two of you on earth agree about anything you ask for, it will be done for you by my Father in heaven. For where two or three come together in my name, there am I with them. (Matthew 18:19–20)

Therefore I tell you, whatever you ask for in prayer, believe that you have received it, and it will be yours. And when you stand praying, if you hold anything against anyone, forgive him, so that your Father in heaven may forgive you your sins. (Mark 11:24–26)

Pray continually. (1 Thessalonians 5:17)

REPENTANCE

Godly sorrow brings repentance that leads to salvation and leaves no regret, but worldly sorrow brings death. (2 Corinthians 7:10)

The Lord is not slow in keeping his promise, as some understand slowness. He is patient with you, not wanting anyone to perish, but everyone to come to repentance. (2 Peter 3:9)

SALVATION

For God so loved the world that he gave his one and only Son, that whoever believes in him shall not perish but have eternal life. (John 3:16)

I am the way and the truth and the life. No one comes to the Father except through me. (John 14:6)

There is no one righteous, not even one. (Romans 3:10)

For all have sinned and fall short of the glory of God. (Romans 3:23)

But God demonstrates his own love for us in this: While we were still sinners, Christ died for us. (Romans 5:8)

Therefore, just as sin entered the world through one man, and death through sin, and in this way death came to all men, because all sinned. (Romans 5:12)

For the wages of sin is death, but the gift of God is eternal life in Christ Jesus our Lord. (Romans 6:23)

If you confess with your mouth, "Jesus is Lord," and believe in your heart that God raised him from the dead, you will be saved. For it is with your heart that you believe and are justified, and it is with your mouth that you confess and are saved. As the Scripture says, "Anyone who trusts in him will never be put to shame." (Romans 10:9–11)

Everyone who calls on the name of the Lord will be saved. (Romans 10:13)

For it is by grave you have been saved, through faith—and this not from yourselves, it is the gift of God—not by works, so that no one can boast. (Ephesians 2:8)

SHAME

As the Scripture says, "Anyone who trusts in him will never be put to shame." (Romans 10:11)

STRENGTH IN CHRIST

I can do everything through him who gives me strength. (Philippians 4:13)

You, dear children, are from God and have overcome them, because the one who is in you is greater than the one who is in the world. (1 John 4:4)

TRUST

Trust in the LORD with all your heart and lean not on your own understanding. (Proverbs 3:5)

But I trust in your unfailing love; my heart rejoices in your salvation. (Psalm 13:5)

We trust in the name of the LORD our God. (Psalm 20:7)

In you I trust, O my God. (Psalm 25:2)

Trust in the LORD and do good. (Psalm 37:3)

But I am like an olive tree flourishing in the house of God; I trust in God's unfailing love. (Psalm 52:8)

In God, whose word I praise, in God I trust; I will not be afraid. What can mortal man do to me? (Psalm 56:4)

TRUTH

I have chosen the way of truth; I have set my heart on your laws. (Psalm 119:30)

But when he, the Spirit of truth, comes, he will guide you into all truth. (John 16:13)

Do not merely listen to the word, and so deceive yourselves. Do what it says. (James 1:22)

Finally, brothers, whatever is true, whatever is noble, whatever is right, whatever is pure, whatever is lovely, whatever is admirable—if anything is excellent or praiseworthy—think about such things. (Philippians 4:8)

Rejoice in the Lord always. I will say it again:

> *Rejoice! Let your gentleness be evident to all. The Lord is near. Do not be anxious about anything, but in everything, by prayer and petition, with thanksgiving, present your requests to God. And the peace of God, which transcends all understanding, will guard your hearts and your minds in Christ Jesus. Finally, brothers, whatever is true, whatever is noble, whatever is right, whatever is pure, whatever is lovely, whatever is admirable—if anything is excellent or praiseworthy—think about such things. (Philippians 4:4–8)*